WAR TO WINDRUSH

BLACK WOMEN IN BRITAIN 1939 TO 1948

STEPHEN BOURNE

JACARANDA

This edition first published in Great Britain 2018 by
Jacaranda Books Art Music Ltd
27 Old Gloucester Street
London WC1N 3AX

www.jacarandabooksartmusic.co.uk

A CIP catalogue record for this book is available from the British Library

ISBN: 978-1-909762-85-5

Book design and typesetting by Rodney Dive

Printed and bound in Great Britain

Acknowledgements

Keith Howes
Linda Hull
The Society of Authors' Foundation
BBC Written Archives
Black Cultural Archives
British Library
Imperial War Museum London
National Archives
Theatre Museum

Special thanks go to the following for their help with this book:

David Hankin for digitally restoring some of the photographs (www.davidhankin.com)

Two friends, the actresses Anni Domingo and Cleo Sylvestre, for supporting this book by providing memories of their mothers, Rosa Domingo and Laureen Sylvestre.

Author's Note

In *War to Windrush* the terms "black" and "African Caribbean" refer to Caribbean and British people of African origin. Other terms, such as "West Indian", "negro" and "coloured" are used in their historical context, usually before the 1960s and 1970s, the decades in which the term "black" came into acceptable use.

Though every care has been taken, if, through inadvertence or failure to trace the present owners, I have included any copyright material without acknowledgement or permission, I offer my apologies to all concerned.

Contents

Contraband Collection / Alamy Stock Photo

Introduction
War to Windrush

In 2016 my book *Evelyn Dove: Britain's Black Cabaret Queen* was published by Jacaranda Books. I had such a good time working with Valerie Brandes, founder and publisher of Jacaranda, and her team, that when Valerie asked me to work with them again I immediately said that I would. I already had a book in mind, which I intended to call *War to Windrush*. I suggested to Valerie that we could publish this in 2018 to coincide with the 70th anniversary of the arrival on 22 June 1948 of the *Empire Windrush* at Tilbury docks, which brought the first wave of post-war settlers from the Caribbean, and also the 70th anniversary of the birth of the National Health Service (NHS) on 5 July 1948.

Over time, the many books, television documentaries and celebrations of *Windrush* since its 40th anniversary in 1988 had overlooked the women passengers. There were very few women on the *Windrush*, but I felt sad that *Windrush* narratives only focussed on the 492 men. In fact, with only a few exceptions, black women have been almost 'written out' of British history. The historian Delia Jarrett-Macauley accurately observed this in 1996 when she said that the black woman had almost lost her place in British history. In 1996 Delia said: "It is hardly ever remembered that she played an active part in the Second World War, in the services, in munitions factories, in the media and in a multitude of other areas of life." When I discussed the proposal for *War to Windrush* with Valerie and the Jacaranda team, as black women they responded positively to my decision to focus the book on black women only, from the start of World War II in 1939 to the arrival of *Windrush* and birth of the NHS in 1948. It was a ten-year period in which black women made important contributions to the British war effort, society in general, and the world of entertainment. Subjects would include the West Indian women who joined the Auxiliary Territorial Service (ATS), African American servicewomen who were based in Britain, those who supported the war effort on the Home Front including the broadcaster Una Marson, popular singers who entertained the public and the troops, such as Adelaide Hall and Elisabeth Welch, and those who were involved in politics, such as Amy Ashwood Garvey, who attended the 1945 Manchester Pan-African Conference.

With *War to Windrush* I hope to provide a 'back-story' to the post-war settlement of African Caribbeans in Britain. In addition to reworking and revising stories from some of my previous books, it includes new information, in biographical chapters, and gives an overview of a period in which black women made an important contribution to British society and culture.

The Turning Point

18 April 1991 was an important turning point in my life. On that date, I attended the launch of a new book called *West Indian Women at War* by Ben Bousquet and Colin Douglas at the Imperial War Museum. The publication of this book was welcomed for, until then, hardly any books had been published about the lives of black women in Britain. By then, there had been one important exception. In 1984 Ziggi Alexander and Audrey Dewjee helped to make it possible for Mary Seacole's 1857 autobiography, *The Adventures of Mrs Seacole in Many Lands*, to be reprinted by Falling Wall Press.

Mary Seacole (1805-1881) was a Jamaican 'doctress' who, in the 1850s, had travelled at her own expense to the battlefields of the Crimean War. However, despite her fame in the Victorian era, she soon became a forgotten figure. Thanks to the reprint of her book, there was renewed interest in her story. Since 1984 Seacole has received the recognition due to her. For example, she is included in the British school history curriculum and in 2004 she was voted first in the 100 Great Black Britons poll. In 2007 English Heritage erected a Blue

Plaque at her former home at 14 Soho Square in Westminster and in 2016 a memorial statue was unveiled opposite the House of Commons in the grounds of St Thomas' Hospital in Lambeth. It is believed to be Britain's first statue in honour of a named black woman.

At the launch of Ben and Colin's book, I had the privilege of meeting for the first time several black servicewomen from World War II. These included the British-born Lilian Bader, who had joined the Women's Auxiliary Air Force in 1941, and Connie Mark, who had served with the ATS in Jamaica. Also at the launch was Nadia Cattouse whom I had already befriended. Nadia had been one of the first black West Indian women to join the ATS in 1943. It was wonderful to be in the company of these extraordinary women who shared anecdotes about their experiences of World War II. They captured everyone's attention with their lively and engaging anecdotes and I realised how little we knew about their lives in wartime. By the end of the evening I concluded that what little I had read about them was not the whole story.

Two years later, Lilian Bader and Connie Mark, with Esther Armagon and Norma Best, were interviewed for a video production called *Caribbean Women in World War II*, made by the Caribbean Ex-Service Women's Association and the Hammersmith and Fulham Video and AV Production Unit. Also in 1993, Connie, Esther and Norma were interviewed for Frances Anne Solomon's superb television documentary *Reunion*, shown in BBC2's *Birthrights* series on 5 July 1993. These resources helped enormously in setting the record straight, with the women telling their stories on camera to captive viewers.

Staying Power

In 1984, the year in which Mary Seacole's autobiography was reprinted, the Marxist journalist Peter Fryer published his acclaimed and ground-breaking book *Staying Power: The History of Black People in Britain.* Since its publication, Fryer's *Staying Power* has come to be regarded as one of the main sources of information about black Britons from history. Peter had been at Tilbury docks in 1948 when the *Empire Windrush* arrived from the Caribbean. He was there to report on this historic occasion for the *Daily Worker*, a newspaper published by the Communist Party of Great Britain. Peter's *Staying Power* was one of the few books around in the 1980s that documented the story of black Britons, and so it was very influential. I bought my copy as soon as it was published and it helped me enormously in my own research.

In 2016 David Olusoga commented in his book *Black and British: A Forgotten History* that he had come across Fryer's book in 1986 and acknowledged it as "a uniquely important book and anyone who has ever written about black history has found themselves referencing it, quoting from it or seeking out some of the myriad of primary sources it drew together." I agree with Olusoga's assessment and I also agree with his claim that Fryer's "eloquent chapters offer guidance and provide orientation through a complex and fractured history. Although not the first work of black British history its impact spread further than most, in part because its publication came at a crucial moment, three years after a wave of riots sparked by hostile policing set ablaze black neighbourhoods of London, Bristol and Liverpool." However, over time, I have come to the realisation that Fryer's book, though exhaustively researched and well written, has some limitations.

Anne Rush, in her article 'Reshaping British History: The Historiography of West Indians in Britain in the Twentieth Century' in *History Compass* (March 2007), acknowledged that *Staying Power* "has been credited with awakening Britons to the fact that black people had for centuries been a part of Britain's society" but she also drew attention to Fryer's focus on people "who had, in some way, been politically active in Britain. In large measure this had to do with available sources – persons who were politically active tended to write more and have more written about them – but it also reflected Fryer's own socialist leanings. In this sense Fryer's work was firmly in the mainstream of the leftist activists who worked on black British history in the 1970s."

Local Publishing

If black people in British history are only acknowledged because they come from political backgrounds then we have a problem because it leaves us with gaps. However, not long after *Staying Power* was published, some of the gaps began to be filled, not by academics, but by the grass roots work of locally based publishing initiatives. For example, in Peckham, where I grew up, we had the Peckham Bookplace, a popular community 'hub' that existed throughout the 1980s and into the 1990s on Peckham High Street. In addition to selling books and periodicals, which appealed to the culturally diverse local community, the Bookplace also provided a safe place for teenagers who were absconding from school. They were encouraged to write poetry and short stories. Some of these were published in pamphlet form by the Bookplace and sold in their shop. Similar local publishing ventures existed in other London boroughs, such as the Notting Dale Urban Studies Centre in west London. Funding could also be raised for booklets like *Forty Winters On*, published in 1988 to commemorate the 40th anniversary of the arrival of the *Empire Windrush*.

Forty Winters On was funded and published by Lambeth Services with support from two newspapers, *The Voice* and *South London Press.*

In Hammersmith and Fulham there existed the Ethnic Communities Oral History Project (ECOHP). The Project was founded in 1987 by ethnic community organisations and funded in part by Hammersmith and Fulham Borough Council. Sav Kyriacou, a development worker, was employed to assist with the work of interviewing local residents. In 1991, at the launch of *West Indian Women at War*, I spoke to its co-author Colin Douglas about my adopted Aunt Esther. She was a mixed-race Londoner, born and raised in Fulham, almost eighty years of age, and still living in the borough. This was the turning point. Colin worked as a press officer at Hammersmith and Fulham Council, and he kindly put me in touch with Sav at ECOHP who invited me to come and talk to him at his office. I discovered that ECOHP had been successfully publishing books about various local BME (Black Minority Ethnic) communities. These included *The Irish in Exile, Passport to Exile: The Polish Way to London* and, in 1989, *The Motherland Calls: African-Caribbean Experiences.*

These ground-breaking publishing ventures encouraged the recording of first-hand testimonies and this led to Sav and ECOHP supporting my first book, *Aunt Esther's Story.* The launch took place on 14 October 1991, just six months after I had met Colin Douglas at the Imperial War Museum. The book was based on a series of interviews I had taped with Aunt Esther since 1989. This was my introduction to a significant way of recording and publishing history that I had not seriously considered before. It departed from the work I was familiar with, such as Peter Fryer's *Staying Power* and, for me, this method reached the heart of the subject by bringing alive the first-hand testimonies of those who had lived the experience, and made the history. It is an approach that has continued to inform my work, though sadly the funding of local publishing has vanished since the end of the 1990s.

Their Long Voyage Home

As far as black British history is concerned, and my involvement in it, 1998 was a fantastic year, a watershed. In addition to my book *Black in the British Frame*, that year also saw the publication of Hakim Adi's *West Africans in Britain 1900-1960: Nationalism, Pan-Africanism and Communism*; Jeffrey Green's *Black Edwardians*; Delia Jarrett-Macauley's *The Life of Una Marson 1905-65*; Sam King's autobiography *Climbing Up the Rough Side of the Mountain*; as well as several *Windrush* books including Vivienne Francis's *With Hope in Their Eyes*; Mike Phillips and Trevor Phillips's *Windrush: The Irresistible Rise of Multi-*

Racial Britain; Windrush: Fifty Years of Writing About Black Britain, edited by Onyekachi Wambu; and Tony Sewell's *Keep Moving On: The Windrush Legacy.*

For myself, the work I had undertaken for almost two decades led to being involved in some extraordinary and rewarding projects. In 1998 the University of London's School of Oriental and Asian Studies commemorated the centenary of the birth of Paul Robeson with a conference at which I gave a paper about Robeson's British films, and at the National Film Theatre I curated a Robeson retrospective called *Songs of Freedom*. The British Film Institute still had its African Caribbean Unit, and I made regular contributions to the Unit's journal *Black Film Bulletin*.

At that time, the BBC still had *its* African Caribbean Unit and so the fiftieth anniversary of the arrival of the *Empire Windrush* in 1998 was celebrated in a big way. Mike Phillips and Trevor Phillips's *Windrush* book included many interviews with survivors of the 'Windrush Generation' and its publication by HarperCollins coincided with an important four-part BBC2 television series, also called *Windrush*, broadcast from 30 May to 20 June 1998. The series was shown in the BBC's *Windrush* season which included other television and radio programmes. These included the Windrush Gala Concert shown on BBC2 on 25 July and recorded at London's Alexandra Palace, the venue for the concert which celebrated 50 years of black British entertainment.

For my part, BBC Radio 2 asked me to research and script a five-part series about the *Windrush*. I called it *Their Long Voyage Home* and it was broadcast from 2-30 July 1998. When I discussed the proposal with the series' producer, Maura Clarke, I suggested that we focus on women and she agreed. In the programmes I had seen and heard so far in the BBC's season, the attention had been given almost exclusively to the men. It concerned me that the voices of women from the 'Windrush Generation' had been almost excluded and it was noticeable that the arrival of *Windrush* at Tilbury was always about the men that came on the ship, and not the women. I also asked for a woman to present the series, and suggested either the actress Carmen Munroe or the newsreader Moira Stuart, but Trevor McDonald had already been offered the job.

For *Their Long Voyage Home*, I suggested that three women be interviewed: Helen Denniston, Pearl Connor-Mogotsi and Brenda Clough. Helen's Jamaican father, Oswald Denniston, affectionately known as 'Columbus', had been a passenger on the *Windrush* in 1948. He had spent his life as a market trader in the Brixton community where most of the arrivals had settled after 1948. She told us: "He was a pioneer but that generation faced a great deal of humiliation and sacrifice to make Britain a better place for their families." Pearl had also arrived here in 1948 and been an important figure in black arts and politics in Britain for decades. Brenda had been born in Guyana in South America and she came here as a teenager at the end of the 1950s. Brenda was the niece of my adopted aunt, Esther Bruce. Interviews with the women were interspersed with songs and poetry readings by black artists covering several decades. These included the calypsonian Lord Kitchener who was a passenger on the *Windrush*, Cy Grant, Edric Connor, Bob Marley, Desmond Dekker, Bob and Marcia, Jimmy Cliff, Eddy Grant and Joan Armatrading. The poets included Grace Nichols and John Agard, who was then the BBC's Poet in Residence. John read 'Windrush Welcome.'

Imperial War Museum

My association with the Imperial War Museum in London began in 2002. For Black History Month in October that year I presented an illustrated talk about Britain's black community on the home front in World War II. The following year I presented a talk about black women in wartime Britain as part of the Museum's *Black Poppies* weekend and to coincide with their *Women and War* exhibition. It was a great success, attracting over 200 attendees including many black women. In 2006 and 2007 I repeated the talk at the Museum for International Women's Week. In 2008 the Museum invited me to join the advisory panel for their exhibition *From War to Windrush* and, at the launch that year, I was reunited with Lilian Bader and Nadia Cattouse, as well as several wartime and *Windrush* veterans I had also befriended including Sam King, Laurie Philpott and Alan Wilmot.

Friendships

In the 1980s I had had the pleasure of befriending some of the women who are featured in *War to Windrush*, and these include Elisabeth Welch, Adelaide Hall, Pauline Henriques, Pearl Connor-Mogotsi and Nadia Cattouse. In that same decade I also met two American legends: Lena Horne, backstage at the Adelphi Theatre in 1984 where she was appearing in her one-woman concert show, and Eartha Kitt, in her dressing-room at the Shaftesbury Theatre in 1988 when she was appearing in Stephen Sondheim's *Follies*. Over a long period of time, these personal friendships and encounters have given me insights into the lives of some of the black women who were living and working in Britain from 1939 to 1948. Trusting me with their stories and, in some cases, sharing their memorabilia, has been a wonderful experience.
I believe the trust came because I refrained from delving into their private lives, and just focussed on their professional experiences. I treasure the letters I received from some of them. Shortly before she passed away,

Pauline Henriques wrote to me about my book Black in the *British Frame: The Black Experience in British Film and Television.* In a letter sent from her Brighton home in 1998, Pauline said:

Congratulations on the publication of *Black in the British Frame* - a splendid title. I am at present immersed in one of the most intriguing books that has come my way and I must offer you special thanks for the Pauline Henriques section. I find myself thrown back into a time that was a thrilling part of my young life. Today (while I am fighting my age-rage) I can sink into the warm memories of my relationships to so many interesting black people: Connie Smith, Edric and Pearl Connor, Errol John and Earl Cameron. I can't thank you enough. So, Stephen, you'll understand why I am filled with admiration for the time and effort you must have put into the book. I am also delighted at the threads of warmth throughout the text. With all good wishes to the successful author: Stephen Bourne.

A few weeks later, Nadia Cattouse also reacted positively to *Black in the British Frame* when she wrote to me:

I like the way you write. You are so deeply interested, never ever patronising the way one or two others can be, and full of insights. You hit the nail on the head when you mention "the wall of silence that surrounds the history of our nations black people." I have long come to the conclusion we will never be a society of real and not 'pretend' people... There is another point you made in connection with the role Paul Barber plays in *The Full Monty*. Let me put it this way. I was grateful rather than sad when I was in [the BBC television drama series] *Angels* that no one tried to create a personal life for my character Sister Young. The scripts, valuable as they all are, were written by people who could not even begin to guess the inner life, the thoughts and feelings the character of an African or Caribbean, or perhaps even an Asian person. Some mean well and bless them for it. That is England.

Sources

Delia Jarrett-Macauley, 'Putting the black woman in the frame', Christine Gledhill and Gillian Swanson (editors), *Nationalising Femininity* (Manchester University Press, 1996)

David Olusoga, *Black and British: A Forgotten History* (Macmillan, 2016)

War to Windrush Diary

1939

3 September
Britain and France declare war on Germany.

17 October
Adelaide Hall headlined a variety concert at the Royal Air Force Station in Hendon. It was the very first wartime concert broadcast live on BBC radio.

1940

3 June
Last British troops and ships leave Dunkirk.

June/July
Rhapsody in Black BBC radio series starring Elisabeth Welch and Evelyn Dove.

3 July
Start of the Blitz against Cardiff.

10 July
Start of the Battle of Britain.

28 August
Start of the Blitz against Liverpool.

7 September
Start of the Blitz against London.

29 December
Major fire raid on the City of London.

1941

3 March Una Marson appointed programme assistant by the BBC to their Empire Service.

28 March Lilian Bader joins the Women's Auxiliary Air Force (WAAF).

7 December Japan attacks Pearl Harbor and declares war on the USA.

1942

October
The first African American servicewomen arrive in Britain. They have been recruited by the American Red Cross.

1943

October
The first black West Indian Auxiliary Territorial Service (ATS) recruits arrive in Britain.

1944

6 June
D-Day. Allied armies land in Normandy.

---

13 June
V-1 flying-bomb (doodle-bug) attacks begin.

---

25 August
Liberation of Paris.

---

8 September
V-2 rocket attacks begin.

1945

29 April
Josephine Baker took part in a victory show at London's Adelphi Theatre.

---

8 May
VE – Victory in Europe – Day.

11 May
Serenade in Sepia starring the contralto Evelyn Dove debuts on BBC radio.

---

15 August
VJ – Victory over Japan – Day.

October
Fifth Pan-African Congress takes place in Manchester. Amy Ashwood Garvey delivers a paper on women's rights.

1946

West Indian Students' Union (WISU) formed in London to promote the interests of West Indian students in Britain.

---

18 July
premiere of the BBC television series *Serenade in Sepia* starring Evelyn Dove.

---

16 September
Pauline Henriques and Connie Smith become the first black actresses to appear on British television in the BBC's adaptation of Eugene O'Neill's *All God's Chillun' Got Wings*.

1947

29 October

Lena Horne arrives in the UK for a two-week variety show at the London Casino.

1948

Two stage productions with black British leading players open in London. The cast of *Native Son* (Boltons, 20 February) included Viola Thompson and Carmen Manley and the musical *Calypso* (Playhouse, 24 May) co-starred Evelyn Dove, Mabel Lee and Cherry Adele.

---

3 June

Katherine Dunham and her dance company (featuring Eartha Kitt) opened at London's Prince of Wales Theatre in *A Caribbean Rhapsody*.

---

22 June

arrival of the *Empire Windrush* at Tilbury docks in Essex marked the first wave of post-war settlement from the Caribbean.

July

The first edition of the black British magazine *Checkers* was published. Edward Scobie, the Dominican-born journalist, was instrumental in getting this published and he promoted it as 'Britain's Premier Negro Magazine'. Hilda Simms, the star of the West End play *Anna Lucasta*, was featured on the cover of the first edition. Sadly, *Checkers* only ran for five issues until January 1949.

---

5 July

National Health Service began.

July/August

Liverpool 'race riots'.

1948 also saw the publications of two ground-breaking British books about 'race': Kenneth Little's *Negroes in Britain* and Peter Noble's *The Negro in Films*.

Owen and Laureen Sylvestre's wedding day in London (1944). Courtesy of Cleo Sylvestre

My Mother's Story
Laureen Sylvestre by Cleo Sylvestre

In 1983, a few weeks before she died of cancer, my mother told me that she had been brought up in a children's home. As we were very close, this came as a complete surprise because she had always led me to believe that she had been brought up by her grandmother. When I asked her to elaborate she wouldn't, but said she'd never told me before as she thought it would upset me. Eight years later, I was appearing at the Theatre Royal in York. An article appeared in the local newspaper and members of my mother's family contacted me. Through them I discovered that there was more to her life than I had ever imagined. Not least, I began to discover what it must have been like to grow up as a mixed-race, illegitimate child in a Yorkshire village during the early part of the last century. I also began to reconsider the history of black people in Britain. Historically, it is generally believed that black people arrived in Britain in the 1950s yet, as a child growing up in London during the 1950s, all the 'coloured' people I knew had been born here. This is my mother's story.

Winifred Laureen Goodare was born in 1911 at 37 Peel Street, Hull and was baptised at St Paul's Church. Her mother, Jessie Goodare, was twenty-two years old. According to the census Jessie was a variety artist, earning 4/- (shillings) a week. Laureen's father was unknown. There is little mention of him in her file from the Children's Society, although at one point he is referred to as "probably an African." On 30 March 1911 she was admitted to All Saints Nursery College, Harrogate. Laureen was described as healthy, good tempered and attractive with nice habits and as having a foreign appearance and being very dark. She was accepted by the Society on 14 August 1912 and was boarded out with a foster mother, Mrs Mary Dinsdale of Burnt Yates, Harrogate.

In January 1917 Laureen was removed from Mary Dinsdale's care as the foster mother felt that the responsibility of looking after a young child was becoming too much for her in her old age. Laureen went to live with another foster mother who lived nearby but missed Mary Dinsdale and repeatedly ran back to her. As a result it was decided to remove her to St Margaret's home in Nidd and she was admitted on 14 February 1917. A letter describes her as happy and settled.

It was common practice for the supporters of the Society to sponsor named children. They would often select a child from a group of candidates presented to them by the Society and would receive chatty reports of their protégée's progress as well as a photograph. In May 1922 Laureen was the beneficiary of money donated by Mrs Carrie Bennett of King's Bromley, Lichfield. She had lost her little girl in December 1919 and sent money on the anniversary of the child's birthday in April. Mrs Bennett could not guarantee regular donations but was anxious to help Laureen as much as she could. She included extra donations to help buy the child nourishing food as she was recovering from scarlet fever in May 1922. Laureen had spent over a month in an Isolation Hospital returning to St Margaret's on 1 June 1922. When the supervisor of St Margaret's was writing to the Society authorities about the sponsor money in May 1922 she described Laureen as a "fascinating clever pickle and a clean, pure, lovable girl."

In 1926 she left St Margaret's to go into service with Mrs Gethin, Cayton Hall, South Stainley near Harrogate. Her wages were £18 per year. In January 1930 Laureen was back at St Margaret's helping in the kitchen. A letter dated 24 January from Mr J H Hayers, the Secretary of the Ripon-Wakefield and Bradford Branch to

Revd. A J Westcott, the Secretary of the Waifs and Strays Society, stated that she was determined to join a coloured troupe of dancers. Laureen had had difficulty in Yorkshire with the public making remarks about her colour and this influenced her decision to seek employment elsewhere in the country. On 14 April 1930 Mr Hayers reported that Laureen had communicated with a Mons Paul, an illusionist, and had made arrangements to work as his assistant in Bognor and then for a season at Morecambe. After that she travelled with him to Cork, Ireland.

Having fulfilled her engagements with the troupe, Laureen moved to London where, in 1931, she worked in a coffee shop in Aldgate. Later that year she took up service again for a Jewish family (The Kauffmans) in North West London, remaining in contact with them until the 1960s. As a child I remember that she would cook the most delicious Jewish food, which she had probably learnt from them. Determined to enter show business, Laureen studied tap in London under Buddy Bradley a well-known black American dancer and choreographer and started working on 'coloured' shows as a chorus girl touring around the UK. Once, when she was in a show in Cork, she was approached by a very old woman who said "Jesus, I haven't seen one of my own kind for years."

Laureen was based in London when she started working at the Shim Sham Club. The Shim Sham was a popular night club in Wardour Street, Soho. It was frequented by the likes of Edwina Mountbatten, the Italian boxer Primo Carnera and musicians playing there included Fats Waller, Nat Gonella and Garland Wilson. Laureen worked there as cigarette girl and also danced in cabaret as one of the four 'Chocolate Drops.' She told me that once when people got up to dance, they would stub out their cigarettes, even if they had only taken a couple of puffs. Laureen would collect them and on her way home would take them to the homeless people who congregated under Hungerford Bridge. It was whilst working at the Shim Sham that she met the conductor Constant Lambert. They began a long affair and friendship which lasted until his untimely death in 1951.

During World War II, Laureen worked at Manchester Square Fire Station in Marylebone. I seem to remember she said she was in the Incident Room recording fires, fallen bombs etc. Whilst there she made two very good lifelong friends. The first was Honor Frost who had a very distinguished career. After attending art school Honor designed ballets. She then was a pioneer in underwater archaeology, working mainly in the Middle East. The second was Daria Hambourg who was one of my godmothers. She was the daughter of renowned concert pianist Mark Hambourg. Daria was a published poet but suffered from mental health issues for most of her life. Laureen didn't elaborate about her time in the Fire Service, but I do remember her telling me that, one night, when she was on her way home, there was an air raid warning. She found an air raid shelter and was surprised that it was empty. In the morning, after the raid was over, she realised why. It had no roof.

In 1944 she married Owen Oscar Sylvestre from Trinidad, a Flight Sergeant in the Royal Air Force, who came to England to fight in the war. Owen had been awarded the DFM which was awarded to non-commissioned officers and men for exceptional valour, courage or devotion to duty while flying in active operations against the enemy. On 19 April 1945, she gave birth to a daughter. I was named Cleopatra Mary. Constant Lambert wrote to Laureen asking if he could be my godfather, which indeed he became. Laureen's marriage to Owen was somewhat rocky. Like many other service personnel from what was then known as, 'the Colonies', Owen was unable to find employment with a commercial airline company, so he enrolled at the London School of Economics. However, he developed a passion for gambling which eventually destroyed the marriage and he and Laureen divorced in 1955.

Throughout the marriage Laureen worked in various jobs from catering at Bridge parties to cleaning and, when I started school in order to be with her during the school holidays, she became an artist's model working in various Art's Schools such as The Slade, Sir John Cass, Chelsea and Guildford. Although having left formal schooling at an early age, she was exceptionally well read and attended adult education classes throughout her life. She studied French, recorder, upholstery, pottery and in her 60s took on a new challenge of silver jewellery making. By then I had begun my career as an actress and Laureen's jewellery proved to be very popular - getting commissions from my colleagues both at the National Theatre and Young Vic. In 1960 Laureen developed breast cancer, and, worried that I would be left orphaned, she wrote to the Registrar in Hull trying to find any members of the Goodare family. As a result, she managed to contact a brother of Jessie (her mother). He was living in Goole with his wife and family and invited us to stay. We received a warm Yorkshire reception and Laureen met many cousins for the first time. Through them she learnt that her mother (my grandmother) had married, then emigrated to America where she set up a dancing school. She never had another child and although she would send money back to England for her nieces and nephews, she never remembered her own daughter Laureen. It was said that one of her dance pupils was Ginger Rogers, but we haven't yet been able to prove it. Laureen's culinary skills stayed with her. She would easily prepare a Chinese meal for twelve or more in the tiny kitchen of the council flat where we lived near Euston. As a teenager when I discovered a passion for the Blues and started going to music clubs, she would rustle up food for various 'poor' musician friends I brought home, including Brian Jones (of the Rolling Stones) and his girlfriend Linda, Mick Jagger and Long John Baldry amongst others. In 2014, Laureen's granddaughter (my daughter) Zoe Palmer won a seed commission to begin a piece based on Laureen's life called *Fosterling*. This work-in-progress was performed at Ovalhouse Theatre in London to great acclaim and at some stage we hope it will have another life.

Laureen died on 3 January 1983 from cancer, aged seventy-one. She never bore any malice or hatred towards her mother who rejected her, or the fact that she was bought up in a home. She had led a rich and creative life.

Rosa Domingo (a student teacher from Sierra Leone) and D A Thomas (a law student) enjoy the view from the balcony of the Colonial Centre in Russell Square, London (1944). A barrage balloon can be seen in the background. Courtesy of the Imperial War Museum (Ref: D0009)

The Two of Us
Rosa Domingo by Anni Domingo

It is true that we never really know a person until they are dead. Only then, when everyone, old or new, friends, colleagues, relatives and acquaintances, congregate in the one place, at the funeral, do we get the almost complete picture. Everyone brings a piece of the jigsaw, with tales of triumphs and failures, joys and sorrows. It is only then that the pieces of jigsaw are put together to complete a mosaic of the deceased one's life. Thus, it was with my mother. I thought I knew a lot about her from stories during my childhood and, later, during the ten years she lived with me, my husband and three children. She was always ready to entertain her grandchildren with stories about growing up in Freetown. On the day we buried her, however, we all learned a lot more about my mother and the amazing life she had led, the people she had met and the things she had done. Some of the stories surprised or shocked us, others made us cry and many made us laugh. In the end, it was sad to know that she had left us, just as we were getting to know her better.

My mother was born Rosamond Margaret Cecilia Harding on 24 May 1924 in Freetown, Sierra Leone, which was then still a British Colony. She was the only child of indulgent parents, Emma Naomi Henrietta and Thomas Festus Joseph Harding. Growing up my mother was known as 'The Empire Girl' by friends and family because of her birth date. Even in 1924 the Empire, on which (it was said) the sun never set, still commemorated the long dead Queen Victoria's birthday and 24 May was designated Empire Day. In celebration, there were patriotic gatherings, church services and special ceremonies. Rosa always felt special and believed that all the celebrations were indeed for her!

Her father, a policeman, died when she was nine, so she and her mother went to live with Rosa's grandfather, Caleb Athanasius Gabbidon. He was a charismatic man, well over six feet tall with a voice as deep as the roots of the country's famous cotton tree. As a very young child I used to be frightened by his very size. It is said that at the end of the 1800s he had left Freetown for the Congo jungle. No one knew exactly what happened there but he came back a rich man. Travelling to England between the wars, he returned with Austin cars to start the first taxi service in Sierra Leone, the first African to own his own car. He also came back with an English secretary, which my mother told me was something seen as outrageous and the talk of Freetown for quite a while. Caleb had a large hall that was rented out sometimes for dances and this was where my mother's love of dancing first started. She would hide in a corner and watch all the dances, longing to join in but was banned by Caleb. Dancing was to become a huge part of her life. Later when she met Dionysius Samuel Soalla-Bell Domingo in England, they became formidable dancing partners. They were renowned, not only in Sierra Leone, but also in the rest of West Africa, for their waltz and foxtrot and their speciality dance, the Highlife, but I jump ahead.

Rosa was a very determined young girl and having decided that it was not much fun being an only child, she persuaded her very generous grandfather to send her to St Joseph Convent School on Howe Street, as a boarder, although the school was less than a hundred yards away. Once she told me that the school was so close to her home she could stand at the dormitory window and shout to her mother at home. In 1942, when she and seven other young women won scholarships to study in England, Caleb was not going to allow his precious granddaughter to travel all the way to war-torn London via a convoy boat alone. He therefore travelled with the girls, as their guardian and chaperone, much to Rosa's chagrin.

In London, although it was wartime with rationing and blackouts, Rosa was able to meet many other students from British Colonies studying in the 'Mother Country'. They would congregate at the Colonial Centre in Russell Square in Bloomsbury to talk, play pool, listen to the radio and make long-lasting friendships. Many photographs were taken of 'Everyday life at the Colonial Centre' and many were lost. Somehow, several photos of my mother were saved and ended up in the Imperial War Museum in London. In one of the photographs, just above Rosa's head, a barrage balloon can be seen, illustrating the fact that the war is never far away. I was delighted when I found out about these photos, never seen by any of us, and they have been used in several books about black Britain, including one of Stephen Bourne's books. I am sure that my mother, who had passed away by the time I learned about them, did not know of their existence or she would have told me about them, but then again, would she?

Besides dancing Rosa was interested in amateur dramatics and singing. In fact, as a child she wanted to train as a singer but Caleb was having none of that and she was persuaded or rather forced to train as a teacher of what was in those days called Commercial Subjects: that is, shorthand, typing, basic accountancy. She was a fine soprano, who later did sing regularly on the radio, at concerts and at many gatherings. She was a fine actress and a leading light in the Freetown Amateur Drama Company when she returned to Freetown. I can still remember spending hours going over her lines with her for various shows. Many who knew her in her younger days informed me that my love of theatre came from her and I'm sure they are right. She certainly was most supportive always of my choice of career and eventually persuaded my father that I should train as an actress. She came to see as many of my shows as was possible and once forgot herself so far as to jump up to announce, 'that's my daughter' when the audience had been particularly appreciative.

My mother met and married my father in England while he was studying to become a shoemaker. I can still remember him designing and making some beautiful dance shoes for Rosa. It was now, in London, during the war that Rosa and Dio started ballroom dancing. They quickly became very proficient. They loved their dancing and were often asked by their dance school to go demonstrate at various tea dances around London, including at the Waldorf and the Savoy. With the arrival of children, Rosa's mother sold everything she possessed and came to England to look after us children and we all lived in rented accommodation in Eversholt Street near Euston Station. When years later I complained about the difficulty of finding anywhere to rent in London my mother would regale me with stories of the even more difficult times they had during the war. The situation was worse after the war with the arrival of many West Indians, especially the Windrush. Some English people seemed to forget that Britain had gone to all the Islands inviting the men and women to come and help the 'Mother Country' in her hour of need. England needed commonwealth citizens not just during the war but afterwards too. There were many jobs to be filled and not enough returning soldiers to get the country back on track. Instead of the welcome the West Indians had anticipated there were many knocks: rough words, admonishments, curses and signs on windows stating, 'No dogs, No Irish, No Coloureds.'

As black people in England were made to feel more and more unwelcome and life became ever more difficult with three young children, my parents began to consider returning home to Freetown. This was precipitated, my mother told me once, by an incident on the number 68 bus. It was the day after George VI died in February 1952, the bus was packed and everyone was in a sombre mood. That was the day my older sister decided to point to a man standing by the bus stop and say quite loudly 'Mummy, Mummy, look, a black man.' As we were the only black people on the bus my mother immediately noticed the interest this remark had engendered. Mum tried to change the subject by saying 'Well, you are black too.' 'No,' insisted sister in her very English tones, 'I'm not black, I'm English.' To the amusement of the entire bus, nothing my mother said could persuade the determined seven-year-old that she could be anything other than just English. It was not possible, in her eyes, to be both English and black. Then one of the ladies piped up, 'Well, she had better learn that she is coloured and always will be no matter how long she stays in this country or how well she speaks the language.' My mother got off at the next stop and walked us children the three further bus stops to our flat. By the time Queen Elizabeth II was crowned in 1953, we were packed up and ready to return to Freetown. My mother got a job teaching shorthand and typing at the Technical Institute College and my father set up his own factory, the Zenith Shoe Factory, at 100 Pademba Road, Freetown.

My parents were people of many parts. Besides the shoe factory my father also ran a record store and the Odeon Cinema in town. In time, my mother and my father were to become the presenters of a very well-known radio programme, called 'The Two of Us.' This was a programme on the local radio, Sierra Leone Broadcasting Service (SLBS). People sent requests for their favourite records to be played with dedications. We were all involved, opening letters, sorting them out, marking the dedications and the required records for Mum to write a script. From the age of about seven I read out all the requests sent in by children. Later, when Freetown had its own television studios, one of the first regular programmes was 'The Two of Us' teaching ballroom dancing. Once again, I was roped in to demonstrate foxtrot, or waltz steps, at a time when all my friends were busy doing the Twist. All that practice did come in useful years later when I auditioned for the world-renowned choreographer Twyla Tharp and was chosen as one of the dancers in the film *Absolute Beginners*.

For a while my mother also ran a 'Charm School' for the beauty contest candidates, in Freetown. Again I was by her side demonstrating how to sit, stand and walk with a book on my head. Of course, many of the girls who did come to the school already had excellent posture, could carry quite heavy loads on their heads for long distances without ever letting anything drop. Rosa taught all four of us that one should never stop learning and growing as a person. When I was six and my youngest brother was still only two, my mother left us with our father and returned to England to study further at Pitman's college. Then when I was at Rose Bruford College of Speech and Drama, training to be an actress, my mother was again in England this time doing a year's course in Oxford. There was another course in Italy and later, just as I was leaving to go work in Australia, she was back in England, this time at Durham University doing another Masters' degree. We learnt our lesson well and once she did complain that she could not work out the time difference to call us all at Christmas as her four children were either working or studying in four different continents: Africa, UK, America and Australia.

My mother taught in various colleges in Freetown and was an examiner for the West African Examining Board for several years. She continued to work well into her seventies and it was the war in Sierra Leone that eventually brought her back to live in England. She made many friends and enjoyed being with her grandchildren but the sudden death of her youngest child was too much to bear. She had always hoped to return to Freetown one day but, unfortunately, this did not happen. My mother passed away at my home in Chatteris, England on 20 January 2005. She had watched me on television that night in an episode of *Holby City*, asked for a cup of tea, drank a little, curled up in bed. When I came back the tea was still warm and she was dead! Very English with her tea. At the funeral, after the stories and the anecdotes, my siblings and I knew what we had to do, to put the final jigsaw piece in place. We honoured our mother's wish and took her ashes back to be buried by her husband's side. Rosa and Dio, 'The Two of Us', together once more.

Hattie McDaniel: More Than a Mammy

During World War II, the most visible black woman in Britain was the character Mammy portrayed by Hattie McDaniel in Hollywood's Civil War movie epic *Gone with the Wind.* Released in America on 15 December 1939, the film's British premiere took place in London on 18 April 1940 at not one, but *three* cinemas. The advertising campaign announced "The Biggest Film of all Time – it takes three West End Theatres to accommodate it!" The cinemas were The Empire, Leicester Square; Ritz (next to the Empire); and the Palace in Shaftesbury Avenue. Just before the British premiere, the film had received more Academy Award 'Oscars' than any other film. The 1939 awards were announced on 29 February 1940 in Los Angeles, California and one of the film's most popular recipients was Hattie McDaniel. She was named Best Supporting Actress for her portrayal of Mammy and this was the first Oscar given to an African American actor. Such was the popularity of *Gone with the Wind* with British moviegoers that it ran for an unprecedented four years at the Ritz and this exposure of Hattie, combined with the film's general release up and down the country, made her the most visible black woman in wartime Britain.

Several British reviewers singled out Hattie for praise. *The Times* noted that she "almost acts everybody else off the screen". *The Monthly Film Bulletin* described her performance as "unforgettable". In *The Sunday Times*, Dilys Powell, one of Britain's most respected film critics, thought Hattie "excellent" and the only member of the "astronomical" supporting cast who didn't appear to be overwhelmed by "the catastrophe of the American Civil War in which they were engaged." Film critics of the time recognised that by the sheer force of her personality, Hattie humanised the one-dimensional mammy caricature created by Margaret Mitchell, the author of the novel on which the film was based.

Mammy found her first representation in the popular fiction, poetry and music of the nineteenth century. Aunt Chloe, the mammy in Harriet Beecher Stowe's novel *Uncle Tom's Cabin* (1852), who is described as having "a round, black, shining face", a "plump countenance" and "a well-starched checked turban", is as good an example as any. Mammy first appeared in films in the period before sound was invented, and these included at least nine versions of *Uncle*

Tom's Cabin between 1903 and 1927. Bossy and cantankerous she may be, but her loyalty to white people is never in question. In the silent era, most black roles were played by white actors in blackface, a rare exception being the final, 1927 version of *Uncle Tom's Cabin* in which she was portrayed by Gertrude Howard.

When Hattie McDaniel arrived in Hollywood in 1932 she found it impossible to avoid being type-cast in films as devoted mammies and maids. However, on many occasions, Hattie breathed life into the one-dimensional mammy stereotype. The characters she played were rarely completely submissive or subservient. In film after film, especially some of the great madcap screwball comedies of the 1930s, she gave such characters as Aunt Dilsey, Mammy Lou, Queenie, Pearl and Delilah a wide range of moods. Admittedly she was always cast as a helpful maid and confidante, a loyal, trusted friend to her white mistresses, but through a remarkable effort of interpretation, her mammies and maids were often opinionated, defiant, hostile, flamboyant, assertive and tough.

When the film producer David O. Selznick was casting his production of *Gone with the Wind*, Hattie was the obvious choice for the role of Mammy. At that time, she was the most versatile black actress in Hollywood. Unsurprisingly in scene after scene Hattie matches Vivien Leigh's spirited performance as the feisty, hot-tempered Southern belle Scarlett O'Hara. In the comedy scenes, audiences laugh *with* Mammy, not *at* her. They recognise that she is in charge and will always have the last word. It was almost as if Mammy was trying to reverse the slave-mistress roles. When Mammy tearfully describes to Melanie (Olivia de Havilland) the tragic circumstances of the death of Scarlett and Rhett's young daughter, she unexpectedly reveals deeper emotions. Hattie's expression of pain and grief is very moving. Until 1939, rarely in Hollywood films had a black actress been given the opportunity to show an emotional range. In this scene, Hattie demonstrated that she could do much more than play the clown. Said Helen Taylor in *Scarlett's Women: Gone with the Wind and its Female Fans* (1989): "Her extended semi-monologue as she climbs the stairs with Melanie…affords the actress the opportunity to display a tragic depth, and melodramatic range which none of her other 'maid' roles allowed." In *Scarlett's Women*, Taylor shared her thoughts on the portrayal of Mammy and drew upon her correspondence with the film's female fans to assess how far Mammy transcended the stereotype. Taylor noted that most of the correspondents approved of Mammy, but added that some of them expressed discomfort at the way Mammy is 'patronised' and made into a comic figure. Taylor felt that David O. Selznick humanised Mammy,

Vivien Leigh and Hattie McDaniel in *Gone with the Wind* (1939)

so that Hattie would have a more significant role in the film. She said:

> Mammy is Scarlett's conscience, counsellor, best friend. She expects – and gets – no gratitude… My correspondents felt warmly towards Mammy. Twenty-two named her as their favourite character and her positive qualities were well recognised. She was seen as exceptionally powerful (something which, historically speaking, she could never be): one woman described her as Scarlett's 'matriarchal support', another as 'the mainstay of Tara', and a third accorded her the historically impossible quality of 'the archetypal aristocrat'. Yet another saw her as 'the eternal mother figure', black or white. She was admired for being 'maternal and loving, dignified and wise', and her 'intelligence' was seen as 'confirming the need for abolition of slavery'.

Despite her efforts, for some African Americans Hattie's presence in *Gone with the Wind* and other movies was an embarrassment to them. The *Pittsburgh Courier*, a weekly black newspaper, denounced *Gone with the Wind* for presenting its black characters as "happy house servants and unthinking, hapless clods." Throughout World War II, several black film celebrities, with the Oscar-winning Hattie at the top of the list, were criticised for perpetuating racist stereotypes. Walter White, who was then the executive secretary of America's most influential black civil rights organisation, the National Association for the Advancement of Coloured People (NAACP), collected complaints from African American servicemen. They had signed up to fight the war against Hitler and fascism. One of them accused Hattie and others of lowering the morale of black servicemen. He said they made them wish "that they were sometimes never even born…I don't like to see my people act as though they were just in America to take up space." A wartime poll published in the journal *Negro Digest* revealed that, while 53 per cent of whites believed that Hollywood films were fair to black people, 93 per cent of the black people questioned thought otherwise. Hattie responded to her critics by proclaiming that she would "rather play a maid and make $700 a week, than be a maid for $7".

When the singer Lena Horne arrived in Hollywood from New York in 1942, under contract to MGM, she felt isolated from her family and friends. The feeling of isolation was made worse when Lena was targeted by black actors who felt threatened by her steadfast refusal to play maids, and her desire to change the stereotypical image of black women in films. Lena later recalled in her autobiography *Lena* (1966) that Hattie was the only black artist who went out of her way to make her feel welcome, and offer her support and friendship:

"She was an extremely gracious, intelligent, and gentle lady…I went to her beautiful home and she explained how difficult it had been for Negroes in the movies…She was extremely realistic and had no misconception of the role she was allowed to play in the white movie world."

Hattie McDaniel died in Los Angeles, California on 26 October 1952 at the age of 57.

Sources

Lena Horne with Richard Schickel, *Lena* (Andre Deutsch, 1966)

Helen Taylor, *Scarlett's Women: Gone with the Wind and its Female Fans* (Virago, 1989)

Stephen Bourne, 'Denying Her Place: Hattie McDaniel's Surprising Acts', Pam Cook and Philip Dodd (editors), *Women and Film: A Sight and Sound Reader* (Scarlet Press, 1993)

Britain Part 1

Stephen Bourne's mother Kathy (extreme left) and his adopted aunt, Esther Bruce (extreme right), at a family wedding in the 1940s

1 Esther Bruce and London in Wartime

Esther Bruce was a working-class Londoner, born before World War I. At the outbreak of World War II, Esther's father tried to persuade her to leave Britain and go and live with his mother and sister in the country of his birth, British Guiana. Esther refused. She was a young woman of twenty-six and had rarely left London, and had never travelled abroad. She wanted to stay with her father and the community in which she had been raised. Though she had been corresponding with her grandmother and aunt in British Guiana, Esther had never met them. Esther looked upon her neighbours in the close-knit Fulham community in which she lived as her extended family. Her neighbours included Mrs. Johnson, or 'Granny', the 'mother figure' who everyone turned to for help.

Esther's father Joseph was a merchant seaman who had left British Guiana to see the world. Esther said he had come to England "on a ship and a prayer". He was a proud, independent man. He left the sea, and married an Englishwoman, Edith

Brooks. They made their home in a predominantly white working-class community in Dieppe Street in the Fulham area of London, and this is where their daughter Esther was born on 29 November 1912. Edith died when Esther was five, and Joseph, who worked as a builder's labourer, raised her by himself. Esther described her father as a proud man who was tough, and could take care of himself. In later years, she spoke with fondness about the community spirit that existed in Fulham before and during World War II: "In the old days the people of Fulham used to be one big happy family and we helped each other. We were poor but people cared about each other. People were friendly and that meant a lot."

When the war started, Esther was given a gas mask but she hated wearing it: "It smelled of rubber. I only wore mine once." The blackout made her laugh: "In the war we had the blackout and you couldn't see each other in the street so if you walked into someone you'd say: 'Sorry mate'. Sometimes it was only a lamp post but you still said sorry! And then you'd laugh at yourself and say: 'What's the matter with me? It was only a lamp post!'"

When air raids started in September 1940, Joseph stayed in the house. Esther said he took a chance, "a lot of people did", but Esther went to the public shelter with her neighbours: "One night we all had to get out of there because the Germans surrounded it with incendiary bombs. They were fire bombs which the Germans were dropping so that others who followed could find Earls Court, which was very close to where we lived. They were always bombing Earls Court and a bomb landed right behind the shelter and didn't explode. Some people said they could hear it ticking. The air raid warden came in and told us we had to get out. I had an old girl sitting near me. That was poor old Mrs. Clark. She said: 'Will you take me to the shelter at the other end of the street, Esther?' I said: 'Of course I will, love.' But it was quite a long way to the other shelter and the Germans were going hell for leather. Bombs were falling everywhere. Mrs. Clark was hanging onto me but we managed to get out of the shelter in Eli Street and went with the neighbours through the air raid and into the one in Hilmer Street. The bombs kept falling and the [anti-aircraft] guns at Earls Court kept firing at them. The noise was terrific. But the other shelter was packed. As for being scared, I just didn't think about it." Esther remembered the friendliness and community spirit that existed during the London Blitz: "You'd be walking along and the air raid siren would go, and people opened their doors and shouted: 'Come in here, love' and they would give you shelter. People are not like that today. During the war people were very friendly. I think the war, in a way, made people friendlier but after the war people changed."

After leaving school at the age of fourteen in 1927, Esther worked as a seamstress. From 1935 she enjoyed working as a dressmaker for Mary Taylor in Chelsea, making dresses for, amongst others, the singer Elisabeth Welch, but in 1941 it became clear that unmarried women were needed for war work. Esther was required to leave her job as a seamstress to register for war work. She went to work as a ward cleaner in Fulham Hospital. In addition to cleaning hospital wards, Esther volunteered to work as a Fire Guard or 'fire watcher'. This position came about because of the night of Sunday 29 December 1940, when the City of London was devastated by incendiary bombs, dropped in clusters to spread fires. Armed with a stirrup pump, a helmet and an armband labelled Fire Guard, Esther's work involved standing on the roof of Fulham Hospital during air raids, and helping to put out any fires caused by incendiaries. It was a dangerous job, and many women who had not enlisted in the services volunteered. She said: "It was dangerous work, and I didn't really want to do it, but when the air raids continued, we knew we would all have to do our bit, and pitch in."

During the war, Esther was transferred from Fulham Hospital to Brompton Hospital where she continued to work as a ward cleaner: "I cleaned three wards and I didn't mop the floor over with a broom or a mop. I had to clean the wards the old-fashioned way. Down on my hands and knees with the polish and the bumper!" In the forces ward they treated servicemen who had been wounded serving with the army, navy and air force. Said Esther: "I had a smashing time in there. The pranks those boys got up to! I had a lot of fun in the forces ward. When the boys knew I was coming back on duty for the evening shift they asked me to bring them fish and chips." After the war, Esther remained at Brompton Hospital and worked for many years in the laundry room where her skills as a seamstress were put to good use. Esther worked there for nearly fourteen years. "That was the best job I ever had. It was really great," she said.

In March 1941 tragedy struck when Esther's father, Joseph Bruce, was involved in an accident in the blackout. During an air raid, he was knocked down and injured by a taxi and taken by ambulance to a hospital in Windsor. He died from his injuries several days later at the age of sixty. The blackout was a significant cause of death and Esther's father was one of 9,169 people killed in traffic accidents in 1941 – the highest figure ever recorded for a single year. Esther was left on her own until she was 'adopted' by her neighbour Mrs. Johnson, affectionately known to Esther and the local community as Granny or 'Aunt Nance'. Esther recalled:

"After Dad was killed, I was left on my own. I'd never lived on my own before and I hated it. So Granny Johnson asked me to come and live with her at 13 Dieppe Street. We'd been neighbours for years and we were going to the air raid shelter together. She said: 'Come over here and live with me, Esther.' It made sense. I moved into 13 Dieppe Street and shared a room at the top of the house with Granny. She was like a mother to me. She was an angel."

Mrs. Hannah Johnson was a mother figure to everyone, and greatly loved and respected. For Esther, Granny was a life saver, and they took care of each other until Granny died in 1952 at the age of seventy-five. Granny's granddaughter, Kathy, lived with them at 13 Dieppe Street, and remembered: "They had a sense of fun and knew how to enjoy themselves. Gran and Esther got on well together, and they were together for a long time. Gran was like a mother to Esther…As far as I can remember Esther was the only black person living in our area. She was part of our community. People knew her. She made friends with everyone. She was always chatting to someone in the street."

Granny's grandson Jack remembered the times he accompanied her and Esther to the 'pictures' during the war: "If I knew they were going I'd ask them to take me. Gawd did I love films. I went about four times a week if my mum gave me the money. We'd usually go to the Red Hall but, if they were full and queuing outside, me and Esther would try and rush Gran across the busy North End Road to where the Regal was located – no mean feat considering Gran's size. We hoped we'd get in to see a film there. The Regal was a lovely art deco style building. Now this you won't believe but it is true. Every time we went to the pictures Gran used to like to sit in the front row so she could stretch out her legs and she wouldn't need to get up from her seat to let anyone pass by. If Esther had taken Gran to see a war film Gran would shout out in the cinema for 'our boys' to 'kill the sods' [the Germans]. She'd holler 'shoot the bleeders!' Esther would laugh out loud and so would our nearby audience, but for a young lad like me I found it all too embarrassing."

Throughout the war, during air raids, it was important that everyone got on with each other, and Esther fondly recalled how Granny took care of her, and how the air raids brought their community together, especially in their local air raid shelter: "When I came home from work and went to the air raid shelter I found Granny cooking our tea. They had fires in there, and stoves, and we'd stay in there the whole evening and all through the night. Granny said, 'What do you want, love? Sausages and a baked potato?' I said: 'Yes. O. K.' We had a good time in the shelter. It was warm. We had sing-songs and bunks to sleep on. When a neighbour came in we welcomed them. Everybody was equal and pulled together. If somebody came into the shelter who we didn't know we said: 'Hello, love. Where do you come from?' We didn't turn anybody away. Sometimes during air raids, the bombs came a bit too close and it got scary, but I don't think the shelter would have stopped a bomb from killing us if one had hit it."

After Esther moved in with Granny Johnson, they shared their rations, but Esther found a way to supplement them. Her grandmother and aunt in British Guiana were helpful when she wrote to them, and asked for help: "Times were hard during the war. Food was rationed. There was no fruit. Things were so bad they started selling whale meat, but I wouldn't eat it. I didn't like the look of it. We made a joke about it, singing Vera Lynn's famous song 'We'll Meet Again' with new words, 'Whale meat again!' Often Granny said: 'We could do with this, we could do with that.' So I wrote to my grandmother and Aunt Carrie in British Guiana and asked them if they could send us food. They were better off than us because the Americans were based there. Two weeks later a bloody great big box arrived. Everything was in it, all sorts of tinned food. After that I asked Granny: 'What grub do we need?' and I sent more lists. We welcomed those food parcels."

In 1944 the Germans sent flying bombs over. They were known as 'doodle-bugs'. The engine had a low, humming sound. Esther recalled: "When I heard it [the doodlebug] I knew I was safe but, when the engine stopped, I wondered where it was going to drop. It was really frightening because they killed thousands of people and a lot of them dropped on Fulham. As soon as the engine cut out I'd say: 'Oh, God, it's stopped. Where am I going?' I'd lay down in the kerb or wherever I was and waited for it to explode. I'd just lay down and hope and pray it wasn't going to go off there." Air raid wardens recorded that thirteen doodlebugs fell on Fulham between 18 June and 2 August 1944 and the last one to fall demolished half of Dieppe Street. Seven people were killed and twenty-seven seriously injured. Esther remembered the incident: "The air raid sirens warned us that doodle-bugs were on their way so off we went to the shelter. We were waiting in the shelter for the all-clear when suddenly there was a terrific explosion and the shelter shook. A doodle-bug had flattened parts of Beaumont Crescent and Dieppe Street! People were killed and many were left injured and homeless. Luckily our house was alright, even though it was number thirteen! We called it 'lucky thirteen' after that! Afterwards the air raid warden wouldn't let us go back home because it wasn't safe. They'd hit the gas mains. We had to stay at the Lillie Road Rest Centre until it was safe to return to our homes."

At the end of the war, Esther took Kathy, then aged fourteen, to see St. Paul's Cathedral. Like so many others, Esther found it hard to believe that St. Paul's had survived the German bombardment of London. For many, including Esther, the beautiful and majestic cathedral symbolised the hope and strength of the British people. "Look at it", Esther said to Kathy. "There's not a mark on it. We're lucky. We've still got half a street, but some poor souls have ended up with nothing."

Friendly and outgoing, Esther found it easy to integrate into the culturally diverse Britain of the post-war years but she was saddened by the Notting Hill race riots in 1958: "It was a terrible time for black people. I didn't think anything like that would ever happen in this country." Esther survived a war against Adolf Hitler and fascism only to witness race-hating teddy boys on the streets of London in the 1950s; Enoch Powell's inflammatory speeches on race in the 1960s; the rise of the National Front in the 1970s; and - one year before she died - the murder of Stephen Lawrence. She believed that "if they'd stopped Enoch Powell and the National Front right at the beginning they wouldn't have got a hold."

Esther Bruce died in London on 17 July 1994 at the age of 81.

Sources

Stephen Bourne and Esther Bruce, *The Sun Shone on Our Side of the Street: Aunt Esther's Story* (Hammersmith and Fulham Ethnic Communities Oral History Project, 1991)

Stephen Bourne and Esther Bruce, *Esther Bruce: A Black London Seamstress* (History and Social Action Publications, 2012)

Homeless people from London's East End, including a black mother and her child, after an air raid in September 1940

2 A Letter to Mr. Churchill

To fully understand the contrasting experiences of working-class black Britons in wartime, we can look to the stories of three black women living in London during the Blitz. Esther Bruce's overriding memory of the Blitz in Fulham in south west London was of friendliness and community spirit. In Marylebone in the City of Westminster, Barbara Carter and her young children were helped by their white neighbours when the Luftwaffe bombed London. Barbara's presence in her local air raid shelter was also seen as good luck. However, the same could not be said of a housewife who was living in poor accommodation in the Camden Town area of north west London.

In 1941 Britain's Prime Minister, Winston Churchill, received a letter from the Camden Town housewife. She described herself as the daughter of an Englishwoman and a West Indian father, and married to a West African who was employed on demolition work. In her letter dated 10 October 1941, she pleaded with the Prime Minister to address the discrimination faced by black British citizens in her community. She asked why black people had to suffer because there were no "decent" places for them to live in. "Can't something be done about coloured peoples?" she asked. "After all, we are British subjects. If this letter is received by you I hope it will not be cast aside."

The letter was not cast aside, but forwarded to the Social Services Department of Downing Street. In a reply to the housewife, also dated October 1941, it is suggested that she make an appointment with John L. Keith, the Welfare Officer in the Colonial Office, to discuss with him the issues she raised. The Oxford-educated Keith had joined the Colonial Office in 1939 and in 1941 he became the Director of Colonial Scholars and head of the student department, a post he held for fifteen years. During the war years, Keith investigated the problems faced by many members of Britain's black communities. He maintained an open-minded and liberal approach to the situations he encountered.

Following the meeting between the housewife and Keith, he drafted a report on 29 October 1941 in which he described her as "an intelligent and sensible woman…She told me about the difficulties which working-class coloured people have in finding decent and reasonably priced accommodation in London." Those that were available were "the worst type of old fashioned and insanitary houses because landlords refused to accept them in other places unless they pay exorbitant rents." She explained that every agent black people approached for a room were refused, while other "nationalities" could get places to live in. She added that black people are insulted by the agents of properties when they apply for better accommodation, ask for repairs to be done to their rooms or reductions in rent. They are told that as they are black, they must be thankful for what they can get.

The housewife also alleged that black people in the Camden Town area were badly treated by air raid wardens and police officers who ejected them from air raid shelters and the tube "as if they were Jews in Germany." Keith advised her to encourage black people who had been subjected to such appalling behaviour to make contact with him or his colleague, Ivor Cummings, at the Colonial Office, and he assured her that he would discuss her complaints with the Chief Warden of the Camden Town ARP and a senior police officer. Keith told the housewife that he was very glad that she wrote her letter to the Prime Minister and hoped that she would keep in touch with him. This she promised to do.

Barbara Carter was born in British Guiana in 1914 and was in Europe with her musician husband, the Guyanese saxophonist Stanley Carter, and their baby daughter, when war broke out. The Carters arrived in England in September 1939 and tried to find a hotel, without success. One commissioner at the doors of a hotel in Russell Square put it bluntly when the Carters heard him say "We don't have niggers here." Stanley spent the war years entertaining the troops at camps around Britain, Barbara volunteered to work as a nursery nurse. Stanley's war service brought him into contact with black service personnel and some of them were invited to the Carter's home in London's Baker Street. Barbara, known as 'Babsy' to her friends, cooked and offered hospitality. One RAF serviceman from the West Indies said: "Our main source of socialising was visiting each other. Babsy's home was one of the principal meeting places. Many would give her name to the Red Cross when they had to go into active service. They had a nickname for her, the 'Black Ambassadress'. She received many telegrams telling of her friends' deaths and injuries in action." When the air raids intensified, Barbara evacuated herself and her children to Wales. After the birth of her third child, Barbara returned to London where she kept her 'open door' policy to black service personnel who wanted a friendly place to visit, eat, and meet other black service personnel, entertainers and academics. After the war she continued to offer support, advice and companionship to black settlers.

Sources

Letter dated 10 October 1941 to Prime Minister Winston Churchill, National Archives, Reference: PRO CO 859 77/1

Jacqueline Harriott, *Black Women in Britain (Women Making History series)* (B. T. Batsford, 1992)

Joshua Levine, *The Secret History of the Blitz* (Simon and Schuster, 2015)

Cleo Laine

3 Cleo Laine: She Can Do No Wrong

In the summer of 1939, just before war broke out, Britain's top film producer, Alexander Korda, recruited black extras for his exotic fantasy *The Thief of Bagdad*, released in 1940. During the war, cinema audiences needed escapism and fantasy films like *The Wizard of Oz, The Thief of Bagdad* and Walt Disney's *Fantasia* provided this. The star of *The Thief of Bagdad* was Sabu, the teenage Indian actor who, in 1937, had been launched into a highly successful film career by Korda. Throughout *The Thief of Bagdad*, many black extras can be seen as sailors, Arabs, hand maidens and citizens of Bagdad. They were an important part of the exotic world created by Korda and they are not demeaned. They wear beautiful costumes and are fully integrated into this extraordinary fantasy world. There was also a brief but memorable appearance by the singer Adelaide Hall who had recently settled in London. She sings the haunting 'Be Still, My Heart' in the garden sequence featuring the beautiful June Duprez as the Princess.

Among the film extras was eleven-year old Clementine Campbell, known as 'Clemmie'. She later became famous as the internationally acclaimed jazz singer Cleo Laine. She was the child of a mixed marriage and had been born in Southall, Middlesex in 1927. Cleo's father was a Jamaican who came to Britain in 1914 and served in World War I. After the war, he dreamed of becoming a professional singer. Her mother was born in Swindon and most of her family disowned her when she married a black man. Said Cleo: "She must have been a very strong and liberal lady or she couldn't have married my father in that day and age. They married and they rowed violently, but they remained together for a long time and loved us very much. My brother, my sister and I were scruffy but loved. I didn't really have a hard childhood although, obviously, because of the colour problem, my parents had a lot of struggle and stress. As a ginger headed person gets called Ginger, I was called Fuzzy Wuzzy. I used to fight back." Cleo's working-class mother also fought back: "I can remember her chasing people with a broom when anything unkind was said about her children. She looked after us like a mother hen."

It was a friend of her mothers who asked permission for Clemmie and her older sister Sylvia and younger brother

Alexander to work as film extras in *The Thief of Bagdad* during their school holidays. Cleo later recalled: "Soon we were earning vast sums of money playing dress-up: two pounds ten shillings a day. This was more money than we as a family had ever had to play with: fifty-two pounds and ten shillings a week! We never knew from day to day if we would be asked to return the next day. When we were told to come again tomorrow big grins would appear on our faces – which might have kept us working a little longer; we were not so blasé as some of the other children on the set. Our smiles kept us in work for three of the happiest weeks of my life, getting up wildly early in the morning to catch the Greenline bus that would take us all to the dream world of Denham Studios."

Cleo and her siblings were dressed as Arab urchins and Cleo said that they saw very little of Sabu, except for one scene when he tipped a basket of oranges over to escape the evil Jaffar, played by Conrad Veidt: "The urchins had to dive after the fruit with glee, helping Sabu to get away in the confusion. I did my whooping and hollering wholeheartedly, flinging myself on the oranges and keeping a couple to eat later." Cleo didn't look upon this experience as work: "just a big giggle…It was like living in another world at Denham where they'd built the city of Baghdad, but I used to carry on the fantasy when I came home by bus and would ask for my fare in a foreign accent!"

Cleo's father never made it as a professional singer, but Cleo recalled that he did work as a busker and sang in the streets: "I didn't know this until I was fifteen or sixteen. I was going out with a young man, and when I introduced him to my father he said: 'Oh! I gave him a penny at Waterloo station the other day!' I was so embarrassed. Then I remembered seeing my father counting pennies on the kitchen table and it all tied in." Cleo's mother ran a boarding house: "My mother always looked after women, so I became conscious early on that women were second-class citizens and they needed to express themselves."

Cleo discovered the joy of singing when she was a child: "I was always a bit of a show-off, and once I decided to sing, it was very difficult to stop me. I remember my mother lying in bed and being either entertained or bored to tears by me performing at the end of the bed. She wasn't allowed to go to sleep before she'd heard all the songs." Cleo said she couldn't remember a time when she didn't feel she was going to become a singer: "At school, when teachers asked me about the work I'd like to do, I always replied that I was going on the stage." She named Fred Astaire as one of her early influences: "He had this quality of not being able to sing but he made the song his and got more out of it quite often than a trained singer would have."

In 1942, Cleo left school at the age of fourteen and had a variety of jobs: "but I always managed to leave before they sacked me." The first of these was in a hairdressing salon: "I was paid seven shillings and sixpence a week, for which I washed towels in the ladies' and men's saloons, swept the floors and handed pins to the accomplished, who were doing sets and perms. I stood watching them, and when they were not too busy, I got a lesson in Marcel waving or wet setting, on a piece of hair fixed to a wig block…I was a dog's-body. It was a cheap way of getting a cleaner. But luckily, I did want to learn, and one of the hairdressers made time for me, teaching me quite a lot in the end." Cleo remained at the hair salon for two years. There followed work as a trainee milliner, "learning how to trim hats", pawnshop clerk and cobbler. She hated most of these jobs. However, she did enjoy her time as a library assistant: "I could sit and read all day."

When Cleo was eighteen in 1946 she married George Langridge, a sailor when they met, who then became a builder: "He was an intelligent, sweet man," said Cleo, "and I was ambitious, which is dangerous if you're not with someone who shares or understands it. We stayed together a long time compared to today because it was harder to divorce." In 1947 Cleo had a son named Stuart who was partly raised by her mother when Cleo pursued a career as a singer.

After the war, Cleo began to attend auditions for singing work. At first, she was optimistic but after being turned down many times, she told herself that "at least I was original, I didn't sound like anyone else, but that also seemed to mean that I wasn't commercial either."

Eventually Cleo's unique tone of voice secured her some gigs at various Labour Club dances which, in 1951, led to a successful audition for John Dankworth's band at the 51 Club in London. She said: "I passed the audition, although I had to have a new name…Clem Campbell sounded like a cowboy act, so we drew names out of a hat till we found one we liked." In 1958 Cleo married Dankworth.

Since 1951 Cleo has become one of the world's most celebrated jazz singers. In the 1997 New Year's Honours List, she was appointed Dame Commander of the British Empire. When Cleo celebrated her ninetieth birthday on 28 October 2017, she was the guest of honour in a celebratory concert at the Town Hall, Birmingham.

In 1975, when James Green reviewed her one-woman show at London's Talk of the Town in the *Evening News*, he said: "Miss Laine combines artistry with the vocal fireworks that allow her to scale the musical Everest of three octaves with ease. Her voice is a musical instrument which she uses in quiet ballads, jazz, scat, blues and some good old swingers. Miss Laine can be regally arrogant or playing for laughs.

The pitch is perfect and the control and range astounding. She can do no wrong."

Sources

James Green, 'Oh, my darling Cleo Laine!', *Evening News* (8 October 1975)

Graham Collier, *Cleo and John: A Biography of the Dankworths* (Quartet Books, 1976)

Nikki Henriques, *Inspirational Women* (Grapevine, 1988)

Cleo Laine, *Cleo* (Simon and Schuster, 1994)

4 Liverpool

By the end of the 18th century Liverpool had become one of Europe's greatest ports because of its involvement in the slave trade. Since the abolition of the slave trade in 1807 (with effect from 1 January 1808), there has always been a black presence in Liverpool. In fact, Liverpool's black community is the likeliest candidate for being the oldest in Europe, though black settlements have existed in other seaports such as London and Cardiff for many generations. According to the historian Ray Costello, what sets Liverpool apart from the other seaports is its continuity. He says that some black Liverpudlians can trace their roots in Liverpool for as many as ten generations. Ray acknowledges the existence of black communities in other seaports, "but there have been gaps, communities dying out only to rise again later." This has not been the case with Liverpool.

Grace Wilkie was born Grace Kie Walker in Liverpool in 1918 to an African seaman, Cratue Walker, and an English mother, Elizabeth Cropper. Soon after she was born, Grace's father left his wife and baby daughter to go to America. He never returned. Elizabeth was descended from the Cropper family of Dingle Bank, an old Liverpool family. In the 1700s, they went to Jamaica and purchased slaves, not for themselves, but to bring them to England, to release them, and find work for them. James Cropper, one of Grace's ancestors, joined the movement to abolish slavery but the Cropper family did not carry on with the liberal tradition, and raised objections to Elizabeth's marriage, in 1916, to Cratue. Grace and her mother were rejected by members of the Cropper family.

When she was interviewed by Ray Costello, Grace remembered what her mother had told her about the 1919 riots, when she was old enough to understand: "She said that all the whites and the blacks were fighting. There was cutting, some got arrested and she was compelled at that time to put me in a tin bath and cover me over with blankets and planks to protect me, because they were throwing bottles and bricks, and anything – you name it – through the windows." To shield them from the violence, the local police took many black families to the safety of a local jail, known as the 'bridewell', in Argyle Street.

Grace was ten years old when her mother died, and it was left to an uncle from Africa to teach various domestic chores to the young girl, such as cooking and cleaning the house. In 1991, when Grace was interviewed in the first edition of the BBC television series *Black Britain*, she recalled: "At school we were taught to believe that Africans lived in little wooden huts. My uncle told me it wasn't so. He said a lot of people lived in the bush, but they did have cities for people to live in." In *Black Britain* Grace described the poverty that existed amongst Liverpool's working classes in the 1930s. Fathers pawned their suits, mothers starved to let their children eat. In 1935 Grace married John Wilkie and raised several children. She remembered giving birth to her son Richard, also known as Derry, during an air raid on Liverpool on 10 January 1941: "I became pregnant in 1940 and there was bombs dropping all over the place, anti-aircraft guns going. It was terrible. And we had to have torchlight to bring my son Derry into the world because that night they dropped a bomb right behind where we lived. The hole in the ground was immense. It took away half the street. A lot of houses went that night. Some people got gassed on their premises and through all this I was giving birth to Derry. There was nothing I could do. There was nowhere I could go. It was a bad bad raid." Derry Wilkie became a musician and in the 1960s he was known in Liverpool as 'The Black Beatle'. He had been inspired by his parents. His father was a guitarist and as a child "I heard my mother singing in the kitchen when she was cooking. It's one of my fondest memories. She'd sing songs by Billie Holiday and the Ink Spots." A Liverpudlian through and through, Grace said: "I belong to Liverpool and Liverpool belongs to me." Grace Wilkie died in Liverpool in 2002.

Dorothy Kuya was also born in Liverpool, the daughter of a West African from Sierra Leone, and a white English mother. Like Grace Wilkie, Dorothy was proud to be a Liverpudlian and she in turn was loved by her community. Dorothy was born in the Granby area of Toxteth in 1933. She barely knew her Sierra Leonean father, but she took the name of her Nigerian step-father, Joseph Kuya, after he married her mother, Josephine, in 1939. Dorothy was involved with her parents in the Colonial Peoples Defence Association, and at a young age she was formulating a political viewpoint that would help to further the cause of black people. As a teenager, Dorothy addressed street corner meetings on a soapbox on behalf of the Communist Party. Interviewed by Ray Costello in *Liverpool's Black Pioneers* (2007), Dorothy recalled:

Being black and being discriminated against politicised me! Looking for an outlet for things I was angry about, even at the age of thirteen, led a friend of my mother taking me to a Young Communist League social in Lodge Lane. That was when I joined the Young Communist League. I was too young to have a membership card; I had to wait until I was fourteen. Race was a constant discussion in our house, as was what was happening in Africa. Lots of things were going on around me. I grew up in a very socially conscious atmosphere at home and in the area where I lived. African seamen were discussing what was happening in what was then their colonised countries. As I got older, I realised that many were involved with the liberation movement, contributing by sending money home or having meetings. There was the Yoruba Association, the Nigerian Association, the Ibo, the Sierra Leone Association and others. Many of these associations had their own buildings which the men had bought with their own money. My dad would get newspapers from Nigeria regularly. Africans are very politically aware and as a family, we were all positively encouraged to read the newspapers, including Reynolds News, which at that time, was considered a very left-wing publication.

After Dorothy left school at the age of 15 in 1948, she was awarded a scholarship to Liverpool College of Commerce for one year. She received a certificate in secretarial work. Whilst in the Young Communist League, Dorothy was thrilled to meet the great African American singer and activist Paul Robeson. This highlight of her young life occurred during his successful concert tour of the United Kingdom in 1949. On 8 May that year, Robeson joined a demonstration for peace and against racial discrimination at St George's Hall in Liverpool. It was estimated that 2,500 people were in attendance. At the event, Dorothy was invited to present a bouquet of flowers to Robeson.

Dorothy told Ray Costello: "I was in the Unity Theatre Youth Choir. We would sing Chinese and Russian songs. The discussions and lectures on Marxism consolidated my understanding of the issues of liberation, colonisation and empire. In those days the Labour movement prided itself in educating its members."

Dorothy Kuya died on 23 December 2013 at the age of 80. In an online obituary, Angela Cobbinah paid tribute to her friend:

For me, Dorothy was like a breath of fresh air, such was her passion and, above all, intellectual honesty. Despite her frustration, she took the long view of change and remained fundamentally an optimist. The race relations industry that arose after the disturbances of the 1980s co-opted many militants from the black struggle and gave them fat salaries and fancy titles. Very quickly, they began sounding less and less radical in their smart suits. Not so Dorothy, who remained true to her principles but found herself eclipsed, in terms of public recognition, by a whole army of careerists. I doubt if this bothered her much, though. People were often taken aback by her seeming abruptness, as I was at first, but this was her stage persona more than anything else. In private she was a warm and generous person, who appreciated down to earth decency in people, whatever their political stripes.

Sources

Ray Costello, *Black Liverpool: The Early History of Britain's Oldest Black Community 1730-1918* (Picton Press, 2001)

Ray Costello, *Liverpool's Black Pioneers* (The Bluecoat Press, 2007)

Angela Cobbinah, 'Dorothy Kuya RIP, 1933-2013' (http://angelacobbinah.wordpress.com, 28 December 2013)

5 Cardiff

At the outbreak of World War II, another of Britain's oldest black communities existed in Cardiff in South Wales. Butetown, situated close to the Cardiff docks, was home to a mixture of nationalities. Some of these were West African and West Indian seamen from across the British Empire who married white women, and raised families. It was in the 1890s that Butetown's black settlers started to build a community and Loudoun Square was the area where most Africans and West Indians lived. Until the regeneration of the area in the 1960s, the popular image of Butetown, or "Tiger Bay", was an immoral hotbed of prostitution, gambling and violence. This racist view was perpetuated by tabloid newspapers and the media in general, but it was always strongly criticised and rejected by the people who lived there. What the media ignored was the strong feeling of solidarity that existed in Britain's most culturally diverse community. Butetown's reputation for criminality was refuted by its citizens. Neighbours left their front doors unlocked during the day, and visiting each other's homes was casual. In Colin Prescod's documentary *Tiger Bay is My Home* (1984), the St. Lucian seaman Kenneth Trotman supported this view when he said: "You never miss your island when you're down in Butetown because everybody lived like one big family. Don't matter what colour you was or where you were from. Everybody was one. I never was hungry once in Cardiff because there was always somebody with a cup of tea, or a parcel of chips. People used to live as one. No selfish people was around then."

World War II brought the community even closer together. The Cardiff docks were bombed from August 1940, and the air raids intensified with the Cardiff Blitz which began on 2 January 1941. Some Butetown children were evacuated, others stayed with their families. Louise Benjamin told Shirley Bassey's biographer John L. Williams: "We would look out over the Channel to Bristol, watch ack-ack guns firing, you could see it all in the sky. We'd go down to the Esplanade and watch. For my mother, with my father at sea, it must have been horrific, but as a child, that was what life was. After a while my mother got very blasé and we went under the stairs. I can remember one night we went under the stairs and my mother had hold of my hair and every time there was a blast she would pull and I was screaming."

Shirley Bassey, aged four at the time of the Cardiff Blitz, recalled in an interview in *Empire News* (19 February 1956): "Mother always used to lock our bedroom door when we were safely asleep but during the big air raid on Cardiff docks a bomb blew the windows in. Grace and Eileen had their faces cut by flying glass and started to scream blue murder. When my mother unlocked the bedroom door, they all scrambled out, leaving me behind, yelling." Eventually Shirley's sisters and brothers were evacuated to the valleys, "leaving me at home with my mother. I missed them but as long as I had my mother I was alright."

Shirley was born in Bute Street, Tiger Bay on 8 January 1937 to a Nigerian merchant seaman, Henry Bassey, and his white wife Eliza Jane, a Yorkshire woman. Shirley was the youngest of seven children and later recalled: "My mother was a housewife – she didn't have time to do anything else, poor thing. She was just bogged down with kids." Shirley remained close to her mother until she died in 1982: "She was quite Victorian in many ways. She was a quiet, Northern woman who didn't give much away about herself and was a great cook. My father was a merchant seaman, so I think I got my wanderlust from him, but I don't know about the voice."

Shirley wasn't raised in Tiger Bay, but in the neighbouring community of Splott, which was also multi-cultural. Her teachers at Moorland Road Primary School, which Shirley attended from the age of five, couldn't help noticing that the child possessed an extraordinary singing voice but, Shirley later said, "everyone told me to shut up. Even in the school choir the teacher kept telling me to back off till I was singing in the corridor!" A classmate recalled her singing 'Can't Help Lovin' That Man' from the musical *Show Boat* with such feeling that she made the teacher uncomfortable.

Shirley knew how to defend herself: "The odd kid at school would call me names, but not for long, boy. But it was not enough to give me a complex, not as it would have been in America." As a young child, Shirley wanted to become a nurse or a model, but she was always singing. In 1970 her mother told the *Sunday Express* "When she was a little girl she was always singing. She used to come home from school at lunchtime to sweep the hall and the stairs and all her friends would stand around outside the open front door listening to her singing while she swept." However, Shirley remembered that she was so painfully shy "I used to do it hiding under a table or in a cupboard." After leaving secondary modern school at fourteen, Shirley felt confident enough to begin singing in workmen's clubs in Cardiff and entering talent contests: "My mother was constantly amazed at where the talent came from – it flummoxes me to this day, but I don't dwell on it…I

Shirley Bassey

never won any of those contests. I always lost to a dog act or someone younger. It's true what they say: never compete with animals or children." At sixteen her professional career was launched. Her rise to fame in the 1950s was rapid and Shirley became an internationally acclaimed singer. Among her greatest successes are her contributions to the soundtracks of three James Bond films when, in the 1960s and 1970s, she assisted in conjuring up worlds of danger and excitement in *Goldfinger, Diamonds Are Forever* and *Moonraker.* In 2000 she was appointed Dame Commander of the British Empire.

Shirley Bassey was not the first young woman from Tiger Bay to join the world of show business. As far back as the 1920s young women from Tiger Bay were attracted to the bright lights of London, and the glamorous worlds of cabarets and nightclubs. Christian "Chrissy" Sinclair was one of them. She was born in Butetown in 1917 to Macdonald Sinclair, who was known as "Danny". He came from Barbados and married his Welsh wife Margaret Lewis in Cardiff in 1909. When Chrissy left school, employment prospects for black and mixed-race girls in the 1930s were extremely limited. However, there were always opportunities to be found in the world of entertainment. Chrissy was drawn to the excitement of the world of nightclubs in London's West End, in and around the streets of Soho near Piccadilly Circus. She became a showgirl, and part of London's 'exotic' night life. Her father, who was born in the Victorian era, was enraged. For him, being a show girl was the same as being a prostitute.

Towards the end of the war, Chrissy was one of dozens of black extras and bit players who were employed at Denham Studios in Buckinghamshire on the film *Caesar and Cleopatra* (1945) starring Vivien Leigh. She also met her husband, Henry Kennard, an African American army corporal based at Wattisham in Suffolk. He swept her off her feet, married her in London on 22 September 1945, and took her to his home in Boston, Massachusetts. Chrissy's nephew Neil takes up the story: "Chrissy was among the first war brides to make the transatlantic crossing. On board the passenger vessel at Southampton was a military band, a ship load of people and the excitement of brides off to new lives. Of course they sang. "Play Jerusalem!" she shouted. And they obliged. "No, no," she exclaimed, "Not that one!" Then she sang, "And did those feet in ancient times..." – and all the British brides joined in. With Chrissy singing "Mae hen 'wlad fy nhadau" the ship departed." Chrissy didn't visit Tiger Bay again until 1958.

Chrissy Sinclair died in Boston in 1986 at the age of 69.

Sources

Neil M. C. Sinclair, *The Tiger Bay Story* (Butetown History and Arts Project, 1993)

Olwen Watkins, 'Black and Welsh', *Black and Asian Studies Association Newsletter*, No. 13 (September 1995)

Muriel Burgess, *Shirley: An Appreciation of the Life of Shirley Bassey* (Century, 1998)

Alan Llwyd, *Cymru Ddu: Hanes Pobl Dduon Cymru/Black Wales: A History of Black Welsh People* (Hughes and Son, 2005)

Butetown Remembers World War II: Seamen, the Forces, Evacuees, an exhibition by the Butetown History and Arts Centre (2005)

John L. Williams, *Miss Shirley Bassey* (Quercus, 2010)

Expatriates Part 1

6 Adelaide Hall Goes to War

In the 1920s New York-born Adelaide Hall was the famous revue star who introduced the popular song 'I Can't Give You Anything but Love' in the long-running Broadway stage show *Blackbirds of 1928*. At the same time, she was a jazz innovator as important and influential as Louis Armstrong and Duke Ellington. They were part of the generation of African American singers and musicians that created the sound of jazz. In 1927 Adelaide's wordless vocal on Duke Ellington's famous recording of 'Creole Love Call' was innovatory as a use of the voice as pure jazz instrument. 'Creole Love Call' is acknowledged as a landmark in jazz history. In the 1930s Adelaide became an international star, with successful appearances in Europe, including her London debut at the Palladium in 1931. She was also a headliner at New York's famous Cotton Club.

In 1924 Adelaide married Bertram Hicks, a Trinidadian seaman and a British subject. He gave up his job in the Merchant Navy to manage her career. However, in America, when Bert accompanied Adelaide on tour, he would impersonate a South American with a Spanish accent. He did this to avoid confrontations with white racists when the tours took them to America's racially segregated southern states. That way he could enter restaurants and buy food for his wife and the musicians in her band. When Bert grew tired of this, he insisted that the couple move to Europe.

In Paris, Adelaide and her husband found themselves embraced by Parisians who were well-known for their acceptance of African Americans, especially those with connections to the world of jazz. The couple opened a popular nightclub which they named La Grosse Pomme (The Big Apple). It attracted famous patrons such as Maurice Chevalier, Charles Boyer and Josephine Baker but, with the threat of war, and the possibility of a German occupation of France, Adelaide and Bert looked towards London for a new home and a new nightclub. They made the move at the start of 1939.

When Adelaide and Bert arrived in London they took over the Old Florida, a popular nightclub situated in Bruton Mews, close to Bond Street and Berkeley Square. They had a small flat above the club, and Bert had an office. Though primarily a private membership club for the armed services, Adelaide's appearances in the Old Florida's late-night revues attracted many stars of the day including visiting Hollywood legends like Fred Astaire and Bob Hope. Members of the Royal family visited too.

Adelaide Hall in her ENSA uniform which she had specially designed for her by Madame Adele of Grosvenor Street, London (1944) Courtesy of Iain Cameron Williams and Kate Greer.

At this time Fela Sowande, a Nigerian pianist and composer, worked as Adelaide's accompanist. In January 1940, a Pathe newsreel captured Adelaide and Fela in a show at the Florida. This historic film now gives us a glimpse of the interior of Adelaide and Bert's popular nightclub, and Adelaide entertaining her customers.

When Britain declared war on Germany, American visitors and residents were advised by their government to return home, but Adelaide wanted to stay. She took a great risk, with the threat of air raids and a Nazi invasion. Adelaide later explained that she remained in Britain because she was married to a British subject, and refused to leave him. However, Bert tried to persuade his wife to return home to her mother in New York but, she said, "I wanted to stay because I liked England and the people here were very good to me. They were very kind. I didn't want to desert them, or my husband. So I stayed."

The war had hardly begun when Adelaide started to entertain the troops. On 17 October 1939, she headlined in a variety concert at the Royal Air Force Station in Hendon. Other artists on the bill included Will Hay, the famous comedy actor, who introduced the show. The BBC broadcast part of the show, the very first wartime concert broadcast live on the airwaves. Part of the production, including Adelaide and the O'Gorman Brothers, was filmed

by British Paramount News, and this newsreel has survived in the Imperial War Museum's collection. In the film, Adelaide can be glimpsed enjoying herself onstage performing a singalong number with the troops, 'I'm Sending You the Siegfried Line to Hang Your Washing On', a variation on the famous wartime favourite, 'We're Gonna Hang Out the Washing on the Siegfried Line'.

Adelaide Hall's contribution to the British war effort is best summarised in a letter sent by Mrs. Florence Cross to the author of this book. During the war Mrs. Cross was a member of the Auxiliary Territorial Service (ATS). A group of them went to see Adelaide give a concert: "During the war a party of us went to see her. Her performance was interrupted by the air raid siren. As we were ATS, from the gun site in Hyde Park, we stayed put as it was an unexpected night off. We thought we would wait till the show started again but it didn't stop! Adelaide sang and sang, the bombs dropped around us, but no one left. She was wonderful. I've never forgotten her. She had such talent."

In Chapter 12, 'Adelaide Hall and the London Blitz', when Adelaide has a premonition, she avoids the bombing of her nightclub during an air raid.

Sources

Stephen Bourne, *Sophisticated Lady: A Celebration of Adelaide Hall* (Hammersmith and Fulham Ethnic Communities Oral History Project, 2001)

Iain Cameron Williams, *Underneath a Harlem Moon: The Harlem to Paris Years of Adelaide Hall* (Continuum, 2002)

Stephen Bourne, 'The Real First Lady of Jazz', *Guardian* (25 January 2003)

Elisabeth Welch signs an autograph at a wartime concert for the troops

7 Elisabeth Welch: Keeping the Home Fires Burning

When Britain declared war on Germany on 3 September 1939, American expatriates and visitors were advised by their government to return home, but the singer Elisabeth Welch decided not to go back. Elisabeth stayed because, she explained, "All my friends were here and I didn't want to leave them."

Elisabeth was born in New York of bi racial parentage. Her father was of African and Native American heritage, and her mother was a white Scottish lass from Leith in Edinburgh with some Irish ancestry. It was illegal for them to marry in New York in 1902. Said Elisabeth: "They found a Catholic priest who married them in secret. My mother was a wonderful woman. She was brave and defiant. I consider such marriage natural, for love has no barriers and should not be hindered by laws." Elisabeth settled in London in 1933 and in 1934 she became the first black woman to have her own series on BBC radio: *Soft Lights and Sweet Music*. By 1939 she was one of Britain's most popular singers, working with equal success in cabaret, variety, radio and television.

Elisabeth regarded herself as American by birth, but English in all other respects. London was her home for seventy years. Off stage she fiercely protected her privacy, living quietly in a flat in Cottage Walk off Sloane Street in Knightsbridge. She stood apart from other African American women entertainers of her generation including the extrovert Josephine Baker. Elisabeth also refused to be racially stereotyped. She projected an image of a glamorous, bejewelled woman of the world.

When war was declared, Elisabeth joined the first concert party to entertain the forces in Britain. The following extract, dated December 1939, is taken from an interview with Elisabeth. It was found in an unidentified newspaper cutting in her scrapbook: "There was one concert for a bunch of R. A. F. [Royal Air Force] boys 'somewhere in Britain.' A little hall was packed. Appearing that night were stars like Evelyn Laye, Frances Day and the Western Brothers. Oh, a terrific company. No theatre in the world could afford to hire the lot of us at once. What a crowd! What wonderful appreciation we got! What a thrill we got out of doing it for nothing! We couldn't help having lumps in our throats."

The London Blitz did not begin until 7 September 1940, but in the early days of the war, before the Entertainments National Service Association (ENSA) was formed, Elisabeth was keen to join some of her show business friends and entertain the troops. She later recalled: "A lot of artists would call up friends and get parties together, sometimes with War Office permission. If we went out of London, transport was laid on for us. I went to Salisbury a lot. Wherever we went the boys were very pleased to see us. Sometimes they were a bit stunned, agog at who was up there on the stage in front of them – people like Vivien Leigh, Kay Hammond and Michael Wilding. Often, we had no stage. I've been on a truck, with a terrible broken-down piano, to sing to about six men on an Ack-Ack site in the middle of nowhere. I don't think they really wanted me to sing – though, as the piano was there, I did – they just wanted somebody to talk to. They were bored, lonely and tense, waiting for enemy planes to come over."

Throughout the war, between many stage, film and radio engagements, Elisabeth kept constantly busy singing to troops and war workers, a job that took her to Royal Air Force hangars, army huts, factories and workshops all over the country. She toured the provinces many times in variety shows: "I spent a season at Blackpool and many weeks in Bristol when that lovely city was under fire," She said. "I played morning shows in Manchester at the Opera House during their terrible blitz. I was under fire at Portsmouth, Cardiff, Liverpool and Leeds, and was in London many times when the place was torn to bits."

In 1941 Elisabeth joined the cast of the West End stage production, *No Time for Comedy.* It opened at the Haymarket Theatre on 27 March after a successful tour throughout the provinces, and performances for the troops at many camps under the aegis of ENSA. The stars of the London version of S. N. Behrman's acclaimed Broadway comedy were Rex Harrison, Diana Wynyard and Lilli Palmer. Elisabeth played Wynyard's maid Clementine, a departure for the singer, for this was her first 'straight' role in the theatre. Elisabeth was attracted to the role because Clementine was just as witty and attractive as the rest of the characters. A review in *The Stage* (3 April 1941) noted: "Elisabeth Welch lends vim and force to her vivacious study of Linda's servant." For Elisabeth, in addition to playing her first non-singing stage role, *No Time for Comedy* was also memorable for another reason. It opened at the height of London Blitz. Elisabeth later recalled:

When the air raid sirens went we stopped and whoever was on the stage went forward and said, "There's an air raid and if anyone wants to leave, please do so." We had to do this because some people were air raid wardens or ambulance drivers and had to be on duty. The houselights would come up and we would hear seats banging as people got up. Then the lights would go down and we would carry on with the show, praying we wouldn't be hit. In plays they did that, in the middle of a dramatic scene. When I look back it's strange to remember how everyone kept on working. Every night I wondered if I would still have a house when I got home. I still have my incendiary bomb shovel, I kept it as a souvenir. London was lovely in the blackout.

In Chapter 13, 'Elisabeth Welch: The Man I Love', Elisabeth's inter-racial love affair with a member of one of England's wealthiest and most influential families is doomed as the war intensifies.

Sources

Richard Fawkes, *Fighting for a Laugh: Entertaining the British and American Armed Forces, 1939-46* (Macdonald and Jane's, 1978)

Elisabeth Welch, "A Night to Remember," *Sunday Telegraph* (29 November 1992)

Stephen Bourne, *Elisabeth Welch: Soft Lights and Sweet Music* (Scarecrow Press, 2005)

Visiting Americans Part 1

8 Home Away from Home

Following the Japanese attack on Pearl Harbour on 7 December 1941, America entered the war and from 1942 to 1945 around three million American service personnel came to Britain. Among them were 130,000 African Americans who were segregated and subjected to an appalling degree of discrimination that travelled with them across the Atlantic. By May 1942 there were only 811 African American GIs in Britain, but by the end of 1942 the figure had risen to 7,315. Until 1942, most white Britons had not met any black people, but during the war most of them encountered the African American service personnel, or at least heard about them. The British public was also confronted with America's racial segregation policies and racist attitudes, especially those held by citizens of the Southern states. Unlike their British comrades, American troops were segregated, and remained that way until 1948 when a presidential order from Harry S. Truman put an end to it.

On their arrival in Britain in 1942, white American troops were cautioned about making racist comments in the presence of the British public, and they had to be instructed about the fact that racial segregation on the scale they had in the United States did not exist in Britain. A 'colour bar' existed in some public places, such as public houses, or hotels, but Britain did not racially segregate the public on transport, or in restaurants, as they did throughout the Southern states of America, and in some of the Northern states. Many British people objected to the appalling treatment of African Americans who, in their opinion, had come to this country to help them fight Hitler and fascism.

Overall, African American servicemen and women were given a warm welcome in Britain. Says Professor Phillip McGuire in *Taps for a Jim Crow Army: Letters from Black Soldiers in World War II* (1983): "It was generally considered – by British public opinion and by American travellers and journalists – that most British people accepted black soldiers as American soldiers without regard to race and color; however, the problem lay in the importation of American racial patterns to Britain by American white troops, resulting in clashes, ideological and physical, between American soldiers. Thus black troops felt that, instead of leaving problems of this sort at home, the [white] Americans tried to instil their ways and actions over here."

In October 1942, one year before the first group of black West Indian ATS recruits arrived in Britain, the American authorities brought over the first African American servicewomen. The popular weekly magazine *Picture Post* (31 October 1942) announced their arrival with a photo spread entitled 'The first coloured service girls get down to work in Britain'. *Picture Post* reported that the five servicewomen had been brought here to run the American Red Cross facilities for black troops stationed in Britain: "Negro troops are already a familiar sight in dozens of towns in Britain. They've fitted into our grey, unexotic background with surprising ease. Now the first coloured servicewomen have arrived – a picked handful who are the vanguard of thousands more now being recruited, kitted up and trained in the USA." The five women were all university graduates with backgrounds in social work. Their main meeting place was the Red Cross Services Club at No. 1 Duchess Street in London and this was officially opened on 24 December 1942. The Club provided bedrooms for sixty men, lounges, movie equipment, reading rooms and dining rooms. In January 1943 the singer Adelaide Hall accepted an invitation to be the guest of honour at the launch of the club.

One of the women, Elizabeth McDougald, was commissioned to write about her experiences of working at the club in the BBC journal *London Calling*. In 'A Bit of Home Away from Home' (28 February -6 March 1943), Elizabeth explained why she had agreed to travel to wartime Britain: "There is an essential harmony in moving with one's generation, in sharing its history and fate. Ours has become a war generation, with its stinging tempo of risks, danger, movement and uncertainty – whether to one's taste or not, there it is. Most important to me in making the decision was a conviction, both deeply personal and professional, of the need for somehow expressing decency, kindness, and generosity – the spiritual values for which our civilisation has struggled for centuries."

Elizabeth described her first impression of England: "My first glimpse of England was your countryside – its neat fields, vegetable gardens, and trim homes…Your beautiful swans which I saw swimming with ducks on a lake in Surrey, startled me." She also commented on the warm welcome she and her group received on their arrival: "We tasted for the first time the unfailing British courtesy and graciousness, which still astonishes us. It seems a miracle that in the midst of war anyone should be concerned with the minor matters and the monotonous ailments which beset all travellers… Passers-by have stopped me in the streets to ask if I were being well treated, and seemed satisfied with an affirmative reply. They need have no such concern. We have been well entertained and have been received with overwhelming hospitality. Many casual encounters with policemen, taxi drivers, and civilians have resulted in apologies for English

Picture Post, October 31, 1942

On Arrival By Air, the Coloured Girls Have Their First Look at Britain

The U.S. army brings over five coloured girls specially to look after the first American Red Cross Club for negro service men. They are the first of hundreds who are being trained for social work among negroes in this country.

THE FIRST COLOURED SERVICE GIRLS GET DOWN TO WORK IN BRITAIN

The first coloured women in uniform have just arrived in Britain. We asked Rudolph Dunbar, the famous coloured musician, to interview them for us.

NEGRO troops are already a familiar sight in dozens of towns in Britain. They've fitted into our grey, unexotic background with surprising ease. Now the first coloured Service women have arrived —a picked handful who are the vanguard of thousands more now being recruited, kitted up and trained in the U.S.A.

These Service girls were flown over here to run the first American Red Cross Club for coloured troops. Of course they have the typical liveliness and humour of the negro; besides that, they are all university graduates with experience of social work and organisation. They have all worked in hospitals, for children's welfare, or for negro societies in America, and two of them are physical culture experts as well.

Henrine Ward, of Chicago, is a graduate of the University of Illinois, and has held big executive jobs all over America, with universities and with the Y.W.C.A. She is already booked for a lecture tour when she returns to the States. Mrs. Sydney Taylor Brown (the only married one) has spent six years as a case worker for a Children's Aid Society in Allegheny. Gladys Martin was Director of Social Service in the largest coloured hospital in the world at St. Louis, staffed entirely by negroes. Magnolia Latimer comes from Georgia in the Deep South, and graduated at the famous negro university of Atlanta. Carol Jarett graduated and did social work in Denver, Colorado. So they have all had first-class education and experience in cities all over the States.

The big question, of course, is "how do they like England?" They seem—genuinely—to love it. They came with their heads full of stories of English stuffiness, English aloofness, English lack of humour. They found friendliness, sympathy, hospitality. Gladys Martin was told in America "that if you tell an Englishman a joke on Saturday, he will burst out laughing in Church on Sunday when he sees the point." But she says she has been "in convulsions of laughter"—with us, not at us—ever since she arrived. Magnolia Latimer is much impressed with our hospitality. Carol Jarett, a High Episcopalian, was particularly pleased to be invited to a Harvest Festival.

These Service girls are part of a coloured unit of the Red Cross which is looking after the welfare of all the negro troops in the area. The Director, George Goodman from Massachussetts, wants negro troops in England to see as much of this country as they can. He is not only arranging for the Club where these girls work to have the best possible facilities and games. He wants coloured troops on leave, or off duty, to have the chance of sightseeing. The Lord Mayor of the town has formed a Committee, with a negro representative, to see that the troops get full facilities for going to sports events, entertainments and cinemas, and for seeing the famous sights of the neighbourhood.

The Club is well equipped, and provides first-class food in the highly-flavoured Southern style—or as much in the Southern style as wartime ingredients allow. The highlight is going to be the dance floor, which is now under construction. (The Lady Mayoress has promised to act as hostess). White Service men are admitted to the Club, and about a dozen have already used it in the short time it has been open, including some from the South. Mr. Goodman wants all serving men to know that they are welcome, regardless of colour.

In all this work of organizing and entertaining, the coloured girls are playing an important part. Their experience and enthusiasm are helping hundreds of negro troops to settle down in their strange surroundings. Their work is proving so successful that many more coloured girls will soon be coming over. Mr. Goodman hopes to open similar clubs all over Britain.

Carol Jarett, of Denver, Colorado

She is a university graduate. For fourteen years she has been engaged in social work.

10

Picture Post (31 October 1942). African American servicewomen arrive in Britain. Courtesy of Getty Images

reserve – 'We're not really unfriendly you know – it's just that we don't talk much' – and also for the inadequacies of wartime England. It makes one feel quite humble. We gradually adopted your tea – a wonderful idea! Tea in the morning, in the afternoon, or any time the idea strikes you. By now we are fierce devotees of the tea system."

Even though the Red Cross Services Club was racially segregated, and open only to African Americans, Elizabeth and her colleagues often befriended servicemen from non-American culturally diverse backgrounds. In *London Calling* she commented that most visitors to the Club came from the United States, "but we encourage visitors from the Forces of the other Allied nations." These included three young men from Ceylon who stayed with them at the Club while waiting to be enlisted. She added: "We are becoming very popular with the West Indians, Africans, and Canadians. Our British friends, especially men in the RAF, are frequent visitors."

Mae Street Kidd was also a member of the American Red Cross, proud to be black (though she could have passed for white), and proud of her uniform. While travelling by train in her Red Cross uniform in wartime America, with her darker-complexioned brother in his Army uniform, Mae was often asked to move from the 'coloured' section of the train to the 'white' section. Mae repeatedly refused, and refused to explain herself, as she later explained to her biographer Wade Hall: "I was a grown woman. I was wearing my Red Cross uniform. My brother was a grown man, wearing his Army uniform. We were a brother and sister going to see our parents before we shipped overseas. We were both American citizens serving our country. We didn't owe anybody an explanation."

Mae supervised a group of African American recruits who travelled on the *Queen Mary* from New York to Southampton in 1943. She later recalled: "I never dreamed that one day I'd be a passenger on board the *Queen Mary* on my way to Red Cross service in England. I was put in charge of seven black women. In fact, I should have been in charge of all 121 Red Cross workers on their way to England because I had the highest title." Mae's position as the assistant director of a Red Cross service club gave her the equivalent military rank of captain: "They said that was in case I should be captured, the enemy would know how to treat me. Nobody else in the Red Cross group had a rank that high. But I was passed over, and a white girl was put in charge of all of us." Travelling across the Atlantic was risky, as Mae recalled: "we almost got torpedoed… the most exciting – and dangerous – incident of the trip was being chased by a German submarine for five days. During that episode our ship had to take a zig-zag course to outmaneuver it."

Mae was made the assistant director of a Red Cross service club for black soldiers in Southampton. The black soldiers were not allowed to mix or socialise with white soldiers in the American army. Mae said: "That's where we fed and entertained soldiers who were waiting to be shipped across the English Channel to the war front… we tried to make things pleasant for the frightened, nervous soldiers who came to the club. They knew that many of them were just a few hours away from fighting and that some of them would never make it home. We tried to take their minds off their worries with music, games, and good food. Most of the soldiers were scared young men who were hoping and praying that they would survive the war and return home to their friends and loved ones. Everything was in short supply, but I learned how to scrounge for my soldiers. After our first dance, a soldier said, 'Mrs. Street, you certainly keep this place jumping.' And that's exactly what I wanted to do because it kept the soldiers' minds off the war that was waiting for them just a few miles away."

Very little acknowledgement has been given to the African American nurses and servicewomen who arrived in Britain during World War II. In January 1941, the American Army opened its doors to black nurses, and more than 500 served stateside and overseas during the war. A few years after the arrival of the Red Cross recruits, in January 1945 the American army permitted black members of the Women's Army Corps (WAC) to serve overseas. An all-black unit called the 6888th Central Postal Directory Battalion had been created and, after their arrival, they were based in Birmingham, and later in France. Over seven hundred African American servicewomen of the 6888th postal unit were sent over. Their job was to route mail to millions of service personnel based in Europe. Much of it had been piling up in English warehouses. With over seven million names in the files, there were thousands of name duplications. At one point the unit had more than 7,500 Robert Smiths in their files! After their arrival, the 6888th wasted no time in ensuring that the troops received their mail. Morale could not be maintained without letters from home.

The commander of the unit was Major Charity Adams who, in August 1942, was the first African American to be commissioned as an officer in the WAC and one of only two black women to hold a wartime rank in the WAC as high as major. In her autobiography, *One Woman's Army* (1989), Major Adams recalled that, when she arrived in England by plane "I had my first view of the English countryside, and it was truly beautiful. It was all snow covered, looking as if scenery had been created by a landscape artist." On arriving in London, Charity said it "was very foggy and the English drove on the wrong side of the road. By the time we had landed and boarded the bus, the fog had burned off and the sun was shining on the snow-covered land." Charity noted that, while her unit observed many things that were strange to them, "we were being observed. We had forgotten how strange we seemed, to military as well as civilian personnel." American military personnel could not believe that African American WAC officers were real. "Salutes were slow in coming and, frequently, returned with great reluctance," Charity recalled. "For most of the military personnel we encountered, accepting any Negro officer in the U. S. Army was hard enough, but accepting Negro women officers was a real burden."

When the unit arrived in London on 28 January 1945, they discovered that their 'minority' status disappeared. Major Adams was impressed by the diversity of the people she saw: "Every conceivable kind of uniform could be seen on the streets, worn by all races, colors, shapes, sizes, sexes, and religious persuasions." Major Adams realised the dangers of being in a war zone. Her unit had arrived in London during the period of the V-2 rockets. She witnessed the death and destruction they were causing: "I think my greatest personal admiration for the English, especially the Londoners, was at this time because they 'carried on' in spite of the V-2 bombs. Each morning when we went out, the streets had been cleared of the damage of the bombs of the night before, and the destruction had been boarded up out of sight from the street."

Their arrival in Birmingham generated a great deal of interest. When they were greeted by Brigadier-General Benjamin O. Davis, the only black general in the American army, it was reported on the front page of *The Birmingham Post* (14 February 1945) that they sung their own words to the marching song "There's a long, long trip we're taking." The unit's parade for Lt. Gen. John C. H. Lee was filmed, and local people turned out in their thousands to watch. They were given a rousing welcome. War correspondent Edward B. Toles informed the readers of the *Chicago Defender* ("*First Wacs Overseas Greeted in Britain*," 27 February 1945): "As trainloads of the smartly dressed women, equipped with full field packs, poured onto the station platform, a 30-piece white army band blared out 'Beer Barrel Polka.' Past the lusty cheers of townspeople and down the blackout streets, the first overseas group of Negro WACS marched to its home." Home was a converted boys' school.

Major Adams and her unit discovered that, in Birmingham, they were the first black women many white people in the city had ever seen and they shattered the stereotypes. *The Birmingham Sunday Mercury* (13 February 1945) commented: "These WACS are very different from the coloured women portrayed on the films, where they are usually domestics or the outspoken old-retainer type…The WACS have dignity and proper reserve."

When the 6888th began work in February 1945, they discovered a huge backlog of mail. They worked three eight-hour shifts, seven days a week and in each shift they handled more than 65,000 pieces of mail. Said Major Adams: "Great quantities of mail, six airplane hangars of Christmas packages especially, had been returned to the United Kingdom from the continent during the Battle of the Bulge [December 1944 to January 1945] when the German troops pushed a huge bulge in the Allied front. One of our first jobs was to get these packages to the troops. The longer we were away from home, the more we understood what had become sort of a motto, 'No mail, low morale.'" Under Major Adams supervision, the 6888th broke all records for redirecting mail.

Several members of the 6888th postal unit married African American men who were also stationed in Europe, while other members identified as lesbian. When Brenda L. Moore interviewed members of the 6888th for her book *To Serve My Country, To Serve My Race* (1996), she said that many of the interviewees acknowledged that there were lesbians in the unit. One of them told Brenda: "Things weren't as open then as they are now. At that time [the homosexual lifestyle] was not open at all, most of it was kept hush-hush." A few interviewees stated that they would have preferred that such lifestyles had never existed. One of them commented: "They tried to stay in clusters; all of their friends in a little unit in and of itself. One buddy got in touch with the other buddies and they formed their own little clique." Dorothy Jones, interviewed by Brenda in 1994, did not have a problem with her lesbian comrades: "I had known lesbians from the time I was a kid. Long before I knew what it was, or even the word…I felt flak from people [members of the 6888th] who didn't understand my approach…Some of the straight people could not understand how I could be friendly with lesbians. But I believe that when you're doing what you consider to be right, don't worry about what other people think about it. So I didn't."

In 1981 nine members of the 6888th postal unit took a nostalgic trip back to Birmingham. It was the first time they had been back to the city since 1945. The women were met by the Lord Mayor and visited the old Birmingham school house where they had been billeted for about five months.

Mae Street Kidd died in Louisville, Kentucky in 1999 at the age of 95.

Charity Adams Earley died in Dayton, Ohio in 2002 at the age of 83.

Sources

Elizabeth McDougald, 'A Bit of Home Away from Home', *London Calling*, No. 177 (28 February-6 March 1943)

The Birmingham Post (14 February 1945)

The Birmingham Sunday Mercury (13 February 1945)

'Tripping Down Memory Lane', *Evening Mail* (Birmingham) (29 April 1981)

Charity Adams Earley, *One Woman's Army: A Black Officer Remembers the WAC* (Texas A & M University Press, 1989)

Brenda L. Moore, *To Serve My Country, To Serve My Race: The Story of the Only African American WACs Stationed Overseas during World War II* (New York University Press, 1996)

Wade Hall, *Passing for Black: The Life and Careers of Mae Street Kidd* (The University Press of Kentucky, 1997)

Britain Part 2

Lilian Bader (1941). Courtesy of Lilian Bader and Adrian Bader.

9 Lilian Bader: Life in the WAAF

Lilian Bader was proud of the fact that three generations of her family had served in the British armed forces. Her father, Marcus Bailey, had served in the Merchant Navy during World War I; Lilian and her two brothers, Frank and James, served in World War II; Lilian married a black British soldier who served in the army and their son was a helicopter pilot who served in Northern Ireland. Lilian was one of the first British-born black women to serve in World War II. She joined the Women's Auxiliary Air Force (WAAF) in 1941, two years before black West Indian women were permitted to leave the Caribbean and join up. But Lilian's journey to the WAAF was a difficult one. The young woman faced many obstacles but she was ambitious and feisty, proud to be British, and determined to contribute to the war effort.

Lilian was born in the Toxteth Park area of Liverpool in 1918 to Marcus Bailey, who came from Barbados, and Lilian, British-born of Irish parents. Lilian was the youngest of three children. After Lilian was orphaned at the age of eight in January 1927, she was raised in a convent where she remained until she was twenty because no one would employ her. Lilian, who had a wonderful sense of humour, proved to be popular with her classmates, and was often top of her class. There were no other black or mixed-race children at the convent, but Lilian possessed a strong personality which she used to overcome prejudice. She said she always had a rebellious streak, "take me as you find me and if you don't like me, too bad!"

Lilian made many attempts to find a job, but often she faced racism at job interviews: "you sit there looking very stoic, pretending you don't care, wishing you were out of it. Nobody would employ me. I realised I had a problem with colour." Eventually Lilian found employment in domestic service but, when the war broke out, she was determined to leave it and join the forces. She began with the Navy, Army and Air Force Institutes (NAAFI), an organisation which had been set up in 1921 to provide recreational establishments needed by the British Armed Forces. At the NAAFI in Catterick Camp, Yorkshire, Lilian was enjoying herself until she was asked to leave when her father's Bajan background was discovered by an official in London. For weeks, her supervisor avoided informing her of this decision, but eventually he had to tell her the truth, and release her. Lilian later explained this came about because of the hysteria in Britain in the early months of the war "when anyone who looked a bit foreign or different was treated with suspicion." Reluctantly, Lilian returned to domestic service and felt embarrassed when a group of soldiers at a gun post expressed surprise that she was not doing war work: "How could I tell them that a coloured Briton was not acceptable, even in the humble NAAFI?"

Lilian was determined to join up after hearing the story of a soldier she had befriended. He had been made deaf from the bombing at Dunkirk and he told Lilian that he kept finding dead bodies on the beach. She said: "That really got to me. I felt guilty I wasn't doing anything. So more than ever I wanted to do something." One-day Lilian heard a group of black West Indian men being interviewed on the radio. When they wanted to volunteer and do their 'bit', they had been rejected by the army, but the Royal Air Force accepted them. Consequently, the resilient and resourceful Lilian tried again, and successfully enlisted with the Women's Auxiliary Air Force (WAAF) on 28 March 1941. She found herself "the only coloured person in this sea of white faces but somebody told me I looked smart in my uniform which cheered me no end."

Lilian's joy at being enlisted in the WAAF was overshadowed by tragedy. Just two weeks prior to enlisting, her older brother, Able Seaman James Bailey, was killed in action while serving in the Merchant Navy: "My brother Jim had been reported missing, but I hoped against hope that he had been picked up as I knew he sailed in convoy. The survivors of his ship, the Western Chief, were picked up, but Jim was not amongst them." In December 1941, Lilian became a Leading Aircraftwoman (LACW) and was soon promoted to the rank of Acting Corporal.

Through an ex-landlady in Yorkshire, Lilian contacted a young British-born mixed-race soldier called Ramsay Bader. He was a tank driver who was serving with the 147th (Essex Yeomanry) Field Regiment, Royal Artillery. He was the son of a soldier from Freetown, Sierra Leone, and an English mother, but he had been adopted at the age of six months and raised by a white family. Lilian and Ramsay exchanged letters and photographs.

Until then, Lilian had rarely met other black people, especially in the forces. Lilian immediately felt attracted to Ramsay: "Even in the ugly khaki battle dress, he looked like an officer. However, I remembered the adage, 'good looking nowt,' and reserved judgement. When my sister-in-law asked me later what I thought, I said he was one of those 'actually' men, in what I thought was a drawling 'RP' accent ['RP': received pronunciation, which means the old-style 'BBC English' without regional accents]. We both had religious backgrounds; his was Methodist though his parents had become Quakers. His voice was low, practically without an accent, and he did not swear or say anything which would destroy the respectable image I had formed. It was a relief to meet a coloured boy-friend for a change. I had met no other coloured WAAFs, and only seen an Indian RAF officer and one coloured airman who appeared fleetingly at Condover."

Lilian and Ramsay were married in Hull in March 1943: "We had a quiet little wedding: no music and no flowers on the altar…My wedding cake had a plaster of Paris top which when removed showed a chocolate or ginger cake! We spent the night at a hotel and Hitler duly celebrated with an air-raid." Lilian's chances of further promotion in the WAAF were curtailed when she discovered she was expecting a baby. She received her discharge papers in February 1944.

On 6 June 1944 Ramsay was one of thousands of soldiers engaged in the D-Day landings. It was an anxious time for Lilian: "For long periods you wouldn't get any news at all from the second front, the Normandy landings, because the mail didn't get through. At one stage, I didn't know if Ramsay was alive or dead but you just kept going and I remember kneeling in the chapel and praying like blazers that Ramsay would be saved. It was a terrible time because you knew some people were going to be killed, and Ramsay couldn't swim! That's what worried me more than anything, but he came through."

Ramsay and Lilian Bader's wedding day (1943). They met while he was a tank driver with the Essex Yeomanry and she was serving in the WAAF. Courtesy of Lilian Bader and Adrian Bader

Lilian and Ramsay had two sons, Adrian and Geoffrey, and she then trained to become a teacher. Ramsay died in 1992 at the age of seventy-three. In 2008, at the age of ninety, Lilian travelled to London with Adrian for the opening of the Imperial War Museum's *From War to Windrush* exhibition.

Lilian Bader died in Dorset on 13 March 2015 at the age of 97.

Sources

Together - Lilian Bader: Wartime Memoirs of a WAAF 1939-1944, published by the Imperial War Museum in 1988.

Ben Bousquet and Colin Douglas, *West Indian Women at War: British Racism in World War II* (Lawrence and Wishart, 1991)

The Forgotten Volunteers (BBC Radio 2, 11 November 2000)

Stephen Bourne, T*he Motherland Calls: Britain's Black Servicemen and Women 1939-45* (The History Press, 2012)

Stephen Bourne, 'Lilian Bader' (obituary), *The Independent* (6 April 2015)

10 Amelia King and the Women's Land Army

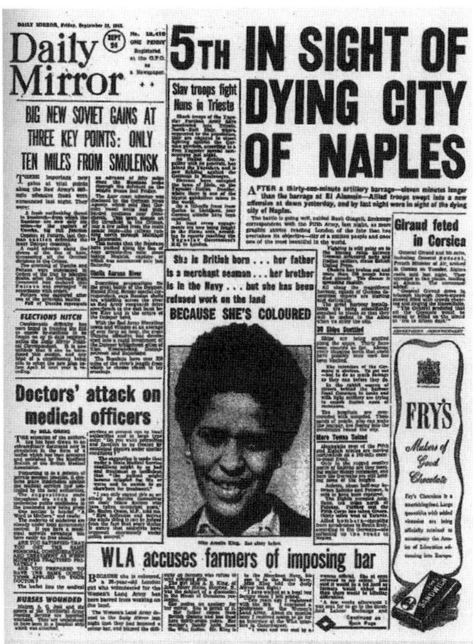

Daily Mirror

5TH IN SIGHT OF DYING CITY OF NAPLES

Slav troops fight Huns in Trieste

BIG NEW SOVIET GAINS AT THREE KEY POINTS: ONLY TEN MILES FROM SMOLENSK

Giraud feted in Corsica

She is British born . . . her father is a merchant seaman . . . her brother is in the Navy . . . but she has been refused work on the land BECAUSE SHE'S COLOURED

ELECTIONS HITCH

Doctors' attack on medical officers

WLA accuses farmers of imposing bar

NURSES WOUNDED

FRY'S Makers of Good Chocolate

Amelia King's story was featured in the *Daily Mirror* (24 September 1943)

In June 1939, the Ministry of Agriculture recreated the Women's Land Army – a throw-back to World War I. By August that year the Women's Land Army had 30,000 recruits. However, when Amelia King, a young black woman from London's East End, volunteered to join the Women's Land Army, she was turned down because of her colour. It was an act of racism that led to coverage in the popular press, which caused outrage by members of the British public who read the story.

Amelia was born in 1917 in Limehouse in the East End of London. Her father, Henry King, from British Guiana, was serving in the Merchant Navy. Later, her younger brothers, Frances and Fitzherbert, both served in the Royal Navy during World War II. So, it is evident that Amelia and her brothers shared a strong moral commitment to fighting the good fight, and serving their King and country. In 1943, Amelia, keen to support the British war effort, applied to the Essex County Committee to join the Women's Land Army. Amelia was interviewed at the offices of the Women's Land Army in Oxford Street, London, but a female official told her that there would be difficulties in finding her a placement because farmers would object to her 'colour' and some of the locals on whom she might have been billeted would also object. Amelia was then sent to meet an official at the Stratford Labour Exchange where she was informed that the Essex County Committee had rejected her for the Land Army. No reason was given, and Amelia was offered a job in a munitions factory. Amelia declined the offer and argued that, if her 'colour' wasn't good enough for the Land Army, then it wasn't good enough for the munitions factory.

Amelia was proud and defiant, someone who fought back. It must have been a difficult decision to make a stand in wartime, when everyone was being encouraged to 'pull together' for the war effort. Yet Amelia persisted and, after a second attempt to volunteer for the Land Army, and then a second refusal, she took her case to her Member of Parliament, Walter 'Stoker' Edwards, an ex-dock worker and Labour Party member. There was press coverage and Amelia made the front page of the *Daily Mirror* on 24 September 1943 which drew attention to Amelia's predicament.

When Walter Edwards confronted the House of Commons with Amelia's story, the Conservative Minister of Agriculture, Robert Hudson, made excuses: "Careful enquiry has been made into the possibility of finding employment and a billet for Miss King, but when it became apparent that this was likely to prove extremely difficult, she was advised to volunteer for other war work where her services could be more speedily utilised." Edwards responded: "In view of the insult that has been passed to this girl and to her father and brother, both of whom are doing valuable war work, cannot the Minister do something about the farmers who are responsible for this position?" Hudson replied: "I do not employ members of the Women's Land Army. It is not like other Women's Services." When questioned, he said that he did not endorse the colour bar. Another MP, Mr. Lawson, told Hudson that "the world listens to matters of this kind, which affect the integrity of the British people", but Hudson made no reply.

The racism experienced by Amelia King aroused feelings of anger in many British people. In one poll carried out by the public opinion organisation Mass Observation, 49 per cent of the 62 per cent who had heard about Amelia 'strongly disapproved' while a further 12 per cent 'disapproved'. A rider was added that said even those who did not entirely believe in race equality were against this particular case of prejudice which was regarded as detrimental to the war effort.

Amelia's story has been documented in several books, including Peter Fryer's *Staying Power: The History of Black People in Britain* (1984), but what happened to her after the racist incident was not researched or documented until her story was included in an edition of the BBC television series *Wartime Farm* on 13 September 2012. The black British historian Caroline Bressey was featured in a short, but informative five-minute sequence of the programme in which she described the wartime experiences of Amelia.

Although no record has come to light of Amelia's point of view, there was a farmer called Alfred Roberts, of Frith Farm in Fareham, Hampshire, who shed some light on what happened to her. He explained in his unpublished memoir that, in 1943, because of the war, he had lost many of his regular staff. When he read about Amelia in the newspapers, he offered her a job on his farm. Mr Roberts was a respected farmer and he held an important position in the County Committee which was responsible for not only overseeing Ministry of Agriculture advice, but also the billeting of volunteers in the Land Army. Amelia was thrilled with Mr Roberts's offer of work, but she insisted on going through the official channels. Amelia also requested formal membership of the Women's Land Army. On 9 October 1943 the *Daily Express* reported that Amelia's requests had been accepted and she took up her position on Mr Roberts's farm with twenty-five other young women. She was also offered accommodation by at least four villagers who lived near the farm. Here is Mr Roberts's memories of Amelia from his unpublished memoir:

I had these delightful Land Army girls around me who were so willing and so happy to work under the leadership of my daughter Betty. I think, about this time, a photograph of a black girl in a field appeared, as a cartoon, and underneath was the inscription, 'All God's Children'. This girl was refused entry into the Women's Land Army as she was coloured. This appeared in the *Daily Express* newspaper. I immediately wrote up the Editor and offered to take this poor black girl. They sent a representative from the *Daily Express* to interview me and I stated that I had no colour prejudice and I wished to take this girl, Amelia King. I was not seeking publicity but I found myself the hero of the hour and a Welsh poet published a poem entitled 'Christian Farmer'. People came to interview me from all over the place. Eventually Amelia King appeared and I rigged her up with a uniform although the Land Army refused to have her. I had in the ranks of the Land Army a good-natured girl called Jessie and she took Amelia King around to all the pubs in the neighbourhood where Jessie and Amelia were the heroines of the hour. This caused more publicity.

In a letter to the author of this book, Mr Roberts's grand-daughter, Hazel Luetchford, who shared the above extract, explained that her mother, Betty, remembered Amelia as a young lady determined to do her bit for the war effort. She was accepted as one of the girls and welcomed with them into the local pub:

Regrettably, as I am sure was the case with other young women who joined the Women's Land Army, she did not realise how hard the work would be, nor how terribly monotonous, though my mother recalls she did work at

Frith Farm for about a year [1943-44]. My grandfather's character – as both my mother and I remember him and more potently may be gathered from his memoirs – was dynamic, energetic, forward-thinking, and charismatic. His attitude to life was 'absolutely can do'. He refused to accept defeat on any problem, no matter how insurmountable it first appeared to be. He thrived on challenge. A great 'people person' he was much loved by those who worked for him for his unorthodox approach to life, his boundless enthusiasm, his practical jokes and his great sense of humour.

Amelia King died in Whitechapel, London in 1995 at the age of 78.

Sources

Peter Fryer, *Staying Power: The History of Black People in Britain* (Pluto Press, 1984)

Peter Ginn, Ruth Goodman and Alex Langlands, *Wartime Farm* (Mitchell Beazley, 2012))

Una Marson and Learie Constantine broadcasting for the BBC's Empire Service in Calling the West Indies (1942). Courtesy of the BBC

11 Una Marson and the BBC in Wartime

Una Marson was one of the most influential women at the BBC in wartime. A feminist, poet, playwright, and social activist, Una had felt inhibited by the lack of opportunities in her colonised homeland, Jamaica, and decided to spread her wings in England. She arrived in 1932, the same year that the BBC launched their Empire Service which would later provide Una with a platform for her programme ideas. In the BBC radio documentary *Voice – The Una Marson Story* (2003), Una's biographer Delia Jarrett-Macauley explained that she was initially drawn to Una through her poetry: "Una Marson was one of the very first people in the Caribbean to start writing poetry in Jamaican patois, but that wasn't the only way in which she was experimenting in verse. Being in London meant having more contact with a range of artists including the Harlem Renaissance poets and reading work of Langston Hughes and Countee Cullen."

After spending some time in Jamaica, Una returned to London in 1938 and found a new home in the leafy suburb of Hampstead. In 1939 she accepted an offer from Cecil Madden, a BBC producer, to undertake some freelance work on his popular television magazine show, *Picture Page*. This work gave Una a stepping-stone into the organisation. The outbreak of war then gave her the opportunity to work for BBC radio and consequently she became the Corporation's first black woman programme maker and presenter. Una's pioneering work for BBC radio spanned just over five years, from April 1940 to December 1945.

During a trial period, Una took part in broadcasts about West Indians and the war effort. These included *The Empire at War* (1 April 1940). She ended one of these broadcasts with the following morale-boosting statement: "I am trying to keep the flag flying for dear old Jamaica in my own way here." Meanwhile, the Empire Service had reached out to English speakers in the outposts of the British Empire or, as King George V put it in the first-ever Royal Christmas Message, "the men and women, so cut off by the snow, the desert, or the sea, that only voices out of the air can reach them." Radio came to the Caribbean in the 1930s and the war helped develop radio broadcasting in the region. It was used to relay news of the war, and to boost morale. Those radio stations relied heavily on the United States radio networks or the BBC for news and entertainment programmes. The BBC's Empire Service helped enormously in this respect.

In March 1941 Una was appointed as full-time programme assistant with the BBC's Empire Service. In April 1941, an article in *London Calling*, described as "the overseas journal of the British Broadcasting Corporation", announced Una's appointment as a member of staff. It described her background and brought home to overseas readers the realities of London in wartime, and how it was impacting on the broadcaster: "She has had the experience of having her house fired by one of Hitler's incendiary bombs, and her spare time is taken up as an air-raid shelter marshal in Hampstead."

Through the popular weekly series *Calling the West Indies*, Una broadcast messages from servicemen and women in England to their families and friends in the Caribbean. Listeners throughout the islands would gather in front of their radios, sometimes up to three times a week, and wait to hear the Jamaican presenter say: "Hello, West Indies. This is Una Marson." Despite the air raids and other wartime dangers, Una and her guests broadcast from a BBC studio and, although it was dangerous, Una understood the importance and value of *Calling the West Indies*. The primary function of *Calling the West Indies* was to enable West Indian servicemen and women to send messages home to their family and friends.

In addition to her work at the BBC, Una took care of many West Indians who had come to Britain in wartime. She provided accommodation in her home which she also offered as a meeting place where they could get together and socialise. Her crowded flat in Bayswater became a centre for lonely West Indian servicemen stationed all over England and Una's sense of humour would dominate the party. She was someone who loved to talk and laugh. Una was very conscious of the struggles faced by West Indians in Britain at that time, and on radio she had the ability to infuse her broadcasts with her personality as well as having a sense of the literary and the cultural.

Towards the end of 1942, Una took part in George Orwell's BBC radio series *Voice*. This enabled poets and novelists to read their work on the air. Afterwards Una devised her own literary series, clearly based on Orwell's format, and in 1943 Una transformed a segment of *Calling the West Indies* into 'Caribbean Voices', a literary item that was influential in shaping the future of the literary development of the Caribbean. 'Caribbean Voices' proved to be a landmark because at that time very few poets and playwrights from the West Indies had been published. It gave them opportunities to raise their profile – and earn some money and it is now recognised as the single most important literary catalyst for both creative and critical writings in the Caribbean. In schools in the Caribbean, students were taught the works of Shakespeare, Dickens, Keats and Yeats. No West Indian writers were acknowledged, and no one was encouraged to write in Jamaican patois. 'Caribbean Voices' helped to change this.

In 1943 Una made an appearance in the short documentary film *West Indies Calling* which was produced by the Ministry of Information. Una Marson was filmed at BBC Broadcasting House in London, hosting *Calling the West Indies* with two Trinidadians, Learie Constantine and Flying Officer Ulric Cross. They described to listeners how people from the Caribbean were supporting the war effort. Film footage provided some rare screen images of black men and women in the services and on the home front. These included service personnel such as fighter pilots, engineers, factory workers, lumberjacks and nurses. The film ended with a dance in a BBC studio and much emphasis is given to cooperation between peoples of different national and racial backgrounds.

In addition to the servicemen and women, in wartime Britain *Calling the West Indies* featured a number of guest appearances by black women who were living and working here. So Una broadcast alongside such famous singers as Adelaide Hall, Elisabeth Welch and Evelyn Dove. Ida Shepley took part in a special programme of greetings and entertainment called *West Indian Christmas Party* in December 1944.

After the war, Una returned to Jamaica and continued to work in politics, broadcasting and literature. In 1998 Delia Jarrett-Macauley's critically acclaimed biography, The *Life of Una Marson 1905-65*, was published. In 2009 a Southwark Heritage Blue Plaque was unveiled by Delia on Una's former home in Brunswick Square, Camberwell, in south east London.

Una Marson died in Kingston, Jamaica on 6 May 1965 at the age of 60.

Sources

Delia Jarrett-Macauley, *The Life of Una Marson 1905-65* (Manchester University Press, 1998)

Voice – The Una Marson Story (BBC Radio 3, 23 July 2003)

Stephen Bourne, *Mother Country: Britain's Black Community on the Home Front 1939-45* (The History Press, 2010)

Expatriates Part 2

12 Adelaide Hall and the London Blitz

Just before the official start of the London Blitz on 7 September 1940, Adelaide topped the bill at the Lewisham Hippodrome in Catford, south London, with her piano accompanist, Gerry Moore. On the evening of Monday 26 August 1940, in the middle of her act, the air raid siren sounded, but most of the audience remained seated. The air raid started and everyone in the theatre could hear the screaming bombs falling and exploding, and the bursts of anti-aircraft machine gun fire. Though the building was strongly constructed, the sound of exploding bombs close by was clearly felt in the auditorium. Adelaide encouraged the nervous audience to join her in some community song numbers and she later recalled: "We – the performers and the audience - were told that no one could leave the theatre because it was too dangerous. Outside everything was burning. So, we had to just carry on and I managed to get the audience to join in many of the songs."

The Stage newspaper noted that the evening's performance ended about 10.45pm and after that, to help calm the audience while the raid continued, Gerry Moore started playing popular music, and Adelaide began singing some extra numbers. *The Kentish Mercury* reported on 30 August that "Miss Adelaide Hall did really wonderful work. She has given several "turns" after the normal programme each night this week. On Monday night the normal programme finished at about 10.50pm and then an impromptu programme was given by Miss Adelaide Hall (12 to 14 songs) ...Members of the audience joined in and then there was a dance. "We kept them amused," said Mr. Vincent, the manager, "and I think they enjoyed it." This procedure was followed on Tuesday and Wednesday nights, when again Miss Hall was the mainstay of the impromptu programmes. A few went home each night but the majority of the audience stayed."

On the night of 26/27 August, for four hours, with bombs exploding outside the Lewisham Hippodrome, Adelaide helped to entertain the nervous audience until the all clear sounded at 3.45 am in the morning. Later that day, Gerry Moore commented that his fingers ached so much from playing that he could hardly move his hands. Though Adelaide could barely speak, in defiant mood she returned to the stage of the Hippodrome the following evening to perform her act as scheduled.

On 14 October 1940, when the London Blitz intensified, Adelaide had a premonition that her nightclub, the Florida, was going to be bombed during an air raid. She told everyone to leave the club before the raid started, but her husband and manager Bert ignored her. He told her that if a bomb had his name on it, it will find him. He stayed, but Adelaide took flight. When the air raid siren warned of an impending raid, Bert took refuge with the night watchman in the cellar where they stored the club's alcohol. As the raid intensified, Bert and the night watchman became increasingly intoxicated. Afterwards he told Adelaide that he couldn't remember anything about the club receiving a direct hit. Bert and the night watchman were saved because they had sheltered in the cellar.

The bombing of the Florida is included in the Air Raid Warden's log which gives the time of the incident as 9.30pm, the type of bomb is described as a high explosive, and the total number of casualties was ten. After losing the Florida, Adelaide worked almost non-stop for the remainder of the war. She broadened her appeal by broadcasting for the BBC and entertaining the troops and factory workers. Audiences loved her because she provided not only glamour, but welcome relief from the miseries, hardships and terrors of war.

Throughout the war, in addition to variety tours, Adelaide entertained in the underground where Londoners in their thousands sheltered from the bombs on makeshift beds on the platforms. She said: "They really loved that. Sometimes you'd sing without music. But it was a challenge – and so rewarding – to get them all singing. And I played all the anti-aircraft sites, including Regents Park which was particularly frightening. The first time I played there an air raid started and, when the guns started blasting, I thought my head was going to be blown off! I'd never heard such a loud bang-bang-bang. I turned to my pianist and asked: 'Are you all right, Ron?' He looked terrified and said, very quietly: 'Just about.' I was singing at another anti-aircraft site in Green Park when we heard the air raid siren. They told me to keep on singing but to stop when I saw the red light. Then we all had to run to the shelter. It was very scary. When we performed during air raids we learned to become philosophical about the dangers we were being exposed to. We'd just go anywhere – within reason."

After losing the Florida, Adelaide and Bert found a new home in Drayton Gardens in the borough of Kensington and Chelsea. Almost every day she observed the devastation caused by air raids: "I saw some extraordinary things during the blitz, like whole buildings which had been destroyed except for small things like a kettle boiling on a stove. That was all that was left. Just a kettle with steam coming out of it!

When we walked the streets, and saw the devastation, we became hardened. We didn't worry too much about the terrible risks we were taking because we wanted to keep up the morale of the troops and the public. Of course, in situations like the one at Lewisham Hippodrome, or another, when I performed in Southampton and the whole front of the theatre was blown away, are a little different. Still, you get to the point, finally, when you say, 'they're coming over again, let's try to carry on,' and we carried on to keep morale from becoming too low."

In a letter to the author of this book, Rosemary Davis remembered her first encounter with Adelaide in 1941: "My father, Fay Davis, was a theatre manager and in 1941 he befriended Adelaide and Bert when she toured for Jack Hylton in a variety show called *Piccadixie*. The Florida club had been blitzed, so Adelaide took to the variety stage and she was terrific. I first saw her at Chatham where *Piccadixie* was playing in my father's theatre. It was a matinee, and the theatre was packed to the rafters! My father made the opening announcement and, while the curtain was still down, you could hear Adelaide's wonderful singing voice off-stage. As the curtain went up, on came Adelaide dressed in white and I shall never forget that wonderful larger-than-life personality. Her act brought the house down. The audience loved her. Afterwards I met her in her dressing-room. She wore a tweed check jacket and skirt, with a beret to match. Then she rushed off to the Royal Naval Hospital in Chatham to entertain the injured troops. I accompanied her and remember her autographing plaster casts! I remained friends with Adelaide until she died. Bert believed in spiritualism and attended meetings. As a couple, Adelaide and Bert didn't contradict each other. They didn't argue with each other. Adelaide really loved him."

In Chapter 18, 'Adelaide Hall Carries On...and Goes to Germany', Adelaide joins the Entertainments National Service Association (ENSA), has a uniform specially tailored for her, and is sent to Germany!

13 Elisabeth Welch: The Man I Love

Elisabeth Welch explained that she stayed in Britain when the war broke out because she had made many friends here and didn't want to leave them. However, there was another reason. She was in love with the Honourable David Astor, a member of one of the wealthiest and most influential families in Britain. Adelaide Hall, another African American expatriate who, in 1939, made London her home, shared this information with the author of this book: "Elisabeth stayed here because she was in love with David and she didn't want to leave him, but it wasn't spoken about. They kept it to themselves."

Before the war, Elisabeth's on-stage appearance of a glamorous, bejewelled woman of the world captivated the young Eton and Oxford educated David Astor. He saw her in cabaret at London's famous Café de Paris in 1935. Elisabeth featured Cole Porter's 'Love for Sale' in her repertoire and David was smitten. However, David's mother was the imperious and formidable Nancy, Viscountess Astor, Britain's first female Member of Parliament. Politically they were incompatible. She was a Tory, he was a Liberal. Unlike his gregarious mother, David was a shy, retiring man. In 2016, Astor's biographer, Jeremy Lewis, described the young David – after he had left Oxford in 1934 – as a young man who turned against his family and social position. Lewis quoted Astor's brother Michael: "For a time he turned abruptly against his own class in society…I resented his experiments at living which seemed to disregard the fragile structure of our society." Nancy Astor had been raised in the American South, at a colonial mansion with a farm near Charlottesville, Virginia. She was the daughter of a Confederate civil war veteran. Growing up, she had been affectionate towards the family's black servants, some of them former slaves. Nancy came to England in the early 1900s for the social and hunting seasons. Vivacious and wealthy she met and married Waldorf Astor in 1906. He was elevated to the Peerage in 1919. Nancy became the first woman in the House of Commons when she won her husband's former seat in Plymouth.

For reasons which have not come to light, in 1944 Nancy invited Walter White to the Astor family's country home at Cliveden in Buckinghamshire. White was the African American civil rights activist who led the National Association for the Advancement of Coloured People (NAACP) from 1931 to 1955. He was visiting Britain in 1944, but the grandeur of Cliveden had less impact on him than Nancy's words.

After luncheon she informed Walter White that Britain didn't have any trouble with the dark-skinned African American GIs who had been stationed in the country since 1942. She described them as "the good black boys". But, she added: "It's the near-white ones that cause the trouble. They're always talking about and insisting on rights." Walter White, who was light-skinned, found himself the object of Nancy Astor's insensitivity when she drew attention to his skin colour: "You are an idiot calling yourself a Negro when you're whiter than I am!"

Despite her background, Nancy's friends did not consider her a racist, but she was unhappy with her son's relationship with Elisabeth Welch. In Britain, mixed marriages were not against the law, as they were in many American states, but in certain social circles, notably Britain's upper classes, it was unacceptable for blacks and whites to marry. Even love affairs were frowned upon. In the 1930s Lady Edwina Mountbatten's extra-marital affair with the West Indian cabaret star Leslie 'Hutch' Hutchinson had shocked upper class 'society'. Understandably David and Elisabeth kept their relationship private, and this was how it remained for the couple in 1939, but the war intervened, and David was drawn into the conflict. He joined the Royal Marines and was wounded in a German ambush in the Ardennes. While convalescing in Italy he wrote to Elisabeth, and the letter has survived. In addition to expressing his feelings for Elisabeth, David mourns the recent execution of his close friend, Adam von Trott, who had been involved in an assassination attempt on Adolf Hitler.

David says to Elisabeth: "How are you? As brave and gay as ever, I hope? I'm sometimes scared of you because if we don't just strike the right note we can jar on each other and that is somehow alarming to me - I think because I'm scared of seeing something I treasured smashed, I mean our relationship. But in my heart I don't believe it ever can be smashed, as like the iceberg, there is far more beneath the surface than one can see above."

David and Elisabeth's relationship did not survive the war. After the war, David married twice, but Elisabeth never married. However, in 1964, Elisabeth took the surname Astor, albeit a fictional one. Her friend Robert Gould wrote an original television musical for her, the enchanting *The Rise and Fall of Nellie Brown*. She played a "Broadway star who took London by storm" and the star's name was Lillabelle Astor.

In 1985, Elisabeth and David renewed their friendship after meeting at a concert. On 4 March 1987, for his 75th birthday celebration at the Waldorf Hotel, Elisabeth accepted an invitation to attend and sing to David, his family and his guests. He died in London in 2001 at the age of 89. Elisabeth always kept silver framed photographic portraits of her mother, and David, taken in 1935, by her bedside.

In Chapter 19, 'Elisabeth Welch Goes to Gibraltar', Elisabeth joins an all-star concert party which includes Edith Evans and John Gielgud, and goes to Gibraltar to entertain the troops.

Sources

Graham Smith, *When Jim Crow Met John Bull: Black American Soldiers in World War II Britain* (I. B. Tauris, 1987)

Jeremy Lewis, *David Astor* (Jonathan Cape, 2016)

West Indian Women in Wartime

West Indian ATS recruits arrive at their training camp in England in November 1943. Courtesy of the Imperial War Museum (Ref: CP 13937D)

14 No Suitable Vacancy

Letter from the War Office to the Colonial Office, London, 8 December 1941:

'...Briefly the Army Council consider that it would be wrong to encourage coloured women to come from the West Indies at their own expense as they would be unused to the climatic conditions and modes of life in England and, in fact, some of them we might not be able to accept. The Council feel, therefore, that any demand by the West Indian women to be enrolled in a uniformed service would be better met by a local organisation.'

Despite resistance from the War Office, black West Indian women were recruited for the services, but not without a struggle and not until 1943, four years into the war. However, it is impossible to know exactly how many of them came to Britain to join the Women's Auxiliary Air Force (WAAF) and the Auxiliary Territorial Service (ATS) in wartime. Different sources give conflicting figures. In May 1943,

Georgy Masson on the cover of *Picture Post*
(4 December 1943). Courtesy of Getty Images

Picture Post, December [illegible], 1943

WEST INDIAN GIRLS JOIN THE A.T.S.

Thirty girls in the West Indies volunteered for the A.T.S. Now they're in Britain—doing their training

WHY have they come to Britain, these thirty girls from West Indies—to a climate as cold as the climate they'd read about—and to a countryside devastated by a winter such as they've never seen? They haven't come because they were in need of a job; in fact, most of them had excellent jobs over there. They're all educated beyond the School Certificate Standard and some of them were school mistresses before they joined up; one was a dressmaker, one a dental assistant, another a radio operator; most of the others were stenographers in lawyers' offices, and department stores, and one was secretary to the Commanding Officer of the South Caribbean Area. Some of them have been to Britain before, and knew what to expect.

For instance, a girl called Georgy Masson was born at Oxford in 1923, left Britain 12 years ago and became a stenographer in the Ford motor depot in Trinidad. And there are some white girls in this party. Patricia Pearce, for instance, used to live in Sussex until her parents decided to go out to the West Indies three years ago, and since then she has been working in the Censor's Office in Trinidad with her best friend, Margery Smith, who has come over with her. This, indeed, is a society without a colour bar, and the coloured girls come over not to be segregated but to join the A.T.S. in a state of equality with all its white members.

Continued overleaf

"The Big City is Slowly Stealing Into My Heart," Says Odessa Gittens

After two days in London, Odessa Gittens (in front) paid it a warm tribute, but now the train is taking her away to her first training camp. She is 32, and taught English and Geography at Christ Church Girls' School, Barbados, before she joined up.

"This Looks Like the End of the Journey": Agnes Scott and Margaret Clairmont in the Truck that Takes Them from Train to Camp

They think the English countryside is as good as the advertisements say, but one thing worries them—why are there no leaves on the trees. The English winter is something they've heard about, but didn't reckon with.

11

when the War Office told the Colonial Office that they would only accept "suitable European women from the Colonies into the ATS", it was declared that around twenty black women were already serving with the ATS. However, it was believed that these women had all been living in Britain before they joined up and had not travelled from the Caribbean. There were also a handful of black women in the Women's Auxiliary Air Force (WAAF) including Liverpool-born Lilian Bader who had joined in 1941.

Most sources claim that, in October 1943, thirty black women from across the Caribbean were the first to arrive in Britain and yet, in 1991, Ben Bousquet stated in *West Indian Women at War:* "381 women actually paid their way across to fight for King and country." Ben added that "They were nice middle-class black women who wouldn't have done anything anyway other than stay at home. So, the war was a form of elevation, a release." Thanks to Ben Bousquet and Colin Douglas's interviews in *West Indian Women at War*, including the Barbadians Odessa Gittens and Marjorie Griffiths, Jamaican Connie Mark and St Lucian Louise Osbourne, as well as those interviewed by Frances Anne Solomon for her superb 1993 television documentary *Reunion*, shown on BBC2, some first-hand testimonies about the experiences of these pioneers have survived.

At the start of the war, the majority of British people had not had any contact with black women from the Caribbean and, if the War Office had had their way, the situation would have stayed that way. In October 1941, Miss L. Curtis, from Bermuda, applied to join the ATS and she was provisionally accepted by the War Office. When it was discovered that she was black, Miss Curtis was informed that there was no suitable vacancy. Joanne Buggins included this story in her excellent article 'West Indians in Britain during the Second World War: a short history drawing on Colonial Office papers', published in the *Imperial War Museum Review No. 5* (1990). She said: "The Governor of Bermuda warned that this rejection would have a most demoralising effect locally, and the Colonial Office was adamant that whatever might happen on the general issue it was quite indefensible that the Department should go back on a definite commitment to Miss Curtis... Only when the Secretary of State for the Colonies, Colonel Oliver Stanley, intervened was this matter settled. The correspondence between the two high level officials is most illuminating, revealing as it does the War Office's intrinsic racism and also that the Colonial Office's principal concern was the impression they were making in the Caribbean colonies."

Joanne Buggins explained that, in a letter to Sir James Grigg, the Secretary of State for War, Colonel Stanley "stressed the importance of bringing black West Indian ATS recruits to Britain, 'the numbers could be very small, all that matters is the gesture.'" When Sir James Grigg reluctantly agreed to Colonel Stanley's request on 19 May 1943, he said: "I don't at all like your West Indian ATS idea. However, my people say they can manage up to thirty in this country without discomfort and as...this will satisfy you, I will agree. But I don't like it."

There was also strong resistance from Lieutenant Colonel W E G Williams, the Assistant Adjutant General who, on 20 March 1943, stated in a letter to the West Indies Department of the Colonial Office that "whilst we are prepared to accept any European women, we cannot agree to accept coloured women for service in this country." However, in 1943, the war had intensified, and this particular 'colour bar' finally came to an end when Colonel Oliver Stanley's request was accepted and black West Indian women were invited to join the ATS. The Americans refused to accept black West Indians so the black West Indian ATS recruits were sent to Britain, while the white West Indian ATS continued to be posted to Washington DC. Once the decision had been made, the response was immediate and some black West Indian women were so keen to 'join up' that they were prepared to pay for their passage to Britain. The first group of black West Indian women who were recruited to the ATS began to arrive in Britain in October 1943 and included Miss L. Curtis.

For their 4 December 1943 issue the popular weekly British magazine *Picture Post* featured Georgina 'Georgy' Masson on the cover, and ran an article about the first thirty recruits. 'Georgy', in her ATS uniform, was strikingly photographed in her ATS uniform for the cover. She was born Marjorie Georgina Masson in Oxford in 1923, but had lived in Trinidad from the age of eight. In the beautifully illustrated article (photographs of the recruits were taken by Leonard McCombe), *Picture Post said:*

Why have they come to Britain, these thirty girls from the West Indies – to a climate as cold as the climate they'd read about – and to a countryside devastated by a winter such as they've never seen? They haven't come because they were in need of a job; in fact, most of them had excellent jobs over there. They're all educated beyond the School Certificate Standard and some of them were school mistresses before they joined up; one was a dressmaker, one a dental assistant, another a radio operator; most of the others were stenographers in lawyers' offices, and department stores, and one was secretary to the Commanding Officer of the South Caribbean Area. Some of them have been to Britain before, and knew what to expect.

Picture Post asked why the women came to Britain, but they were all determined to support the British war effort because they were British subjects. Some of them also saw recruitment as a way out of the oppressive life they were expected to lead in the colonies. Ben Bousquet and Colin Douglas observed that the Barbadian Marjorie Griffiths left home to join the ATS because for her "the war was an adventure. That is not to say that she was not aware of the serious side to the conflict, and what the fighting was about. But her overwhelming memory is of being able to meet people, and see places she would not have come across had it not been for the war."

The following three chapters focus on the individual stories of women who served in the ATS in World War II: Nadia Cattouse, Norma Best and Connie Mark. Connie didn't come to Britain. She served in Jamaica and her story offers a Caribbean perspective.

Sources

Joanne Buggins, 'West Indians in Britain during the Second World War: a short history drawing on Colonial Office papers', *Imperial War Museum Review No. 5* (1990)

Ben Bousquet and Colin Douglas, *West Indian Women at War: British Racism in World War II* (Lawrence and Wishart, 1991)

Birthrights: Reunion, BBC2, 5 July 1993

Caribbean Women in World War II (Caribbean Ex-Service Women's Association and Hammersmith and Fulham Video and AV Production Unit, 1993)

'Historical Documents', *Black and Asian Studies Association Newsletter,* No. 12 (April 1995)

Cecily Jones, 'West Indian Women at War', David Dabydeen, John Gilmore and Cecily Jones (editors), *The Oxford Companion to Black British History* (Oxford University Press, 2007)

Nadia Cattouse in Scotland. Courtesy of Nadia Cattouse

15 Nadia Cattouse: Keep Smiling Through

Nadia Cattouse summarised why black West Indian women volunteered and joined up: "When I was at school there were some books called Royal Readers and these books taught you all about England but nothing about your own country. Then the war began and the men started to go. I had an uncle in a forestry unit in Scotland, and cousins in the RAF. So, when they asked for women volunteers, I wanted to support our mother country too. I was so eager I jumped on my bike straight away to get to Drill Hall." Nadia, who came from British Honduras (now Belize), which was a British colony in Central America, was one of the first black West Indian women to volunteer for the Auxiliary Territorial Service (ATS) when the 'colour bar' was lifted in 1943.

At the age of nineteen, Nadia was signed up immediately and joined a small group of other black West Indian volunteers to travel to Britain, but they had a lot of travelling to do before they reached their destination. Their first stop – in November 1943 - was Jamaica, where they had initial training, but then they had to go via Miami in Florida before passing through Washington DC and sailing from New York to Gourock in the West of Scotland. The young women were unprepared for the racism they encountered on this important journey.

In Miami, the hotel booked for them by the British Army refused to take them. The hotel owner had not been informed that the six women would be black. Said Nadia: "They kept saying we don't want Jamaicans, and it was a few minutes before we realised that what they were really saying was that they don't take black people. We asked the coach driver to help us find a hotel room where we could stay and he said yes and he took us to a hotel. Unfortunately, it was a very seedy sort of brothel place." The following day an ATS officer arrived from Washington and took the women to another hotel where the manager was a Scotsman. He agreed to take them, if they did not enter his hotel by the front entrance. Nadia said: "We were angry, upset and surprised but by the time we were to board the train, we had become very determined girls indeed."

At the railway station, there were two queues for the Washington train: one for whites; the other for blacks. Unused to racial segregation in the West Indies, the women defiantly joined the white queue. The African Americans they encountered in the "Jim Crow" (racially segregated) queue expressed their concerns that something bad could happen to the women. On the train, which was also racially segregated, a compromise was reached when the ticket collector discovered that the six women had sat in a part of the train reserved for white passengers. The women refused to compromise. Helped by a Scottish ATS Officer, they insisted they would only move if they were given first-class seats. Nadia and her fellow travellers were given a drawing-room to themselves: "We refused to go to the Jim Crow car, and the black passengers who befriended us feared for our safety. Our defiant action predated Rosa Parks's refusal to give up her seat on a Jim Crow bus by at least ten years. Her stand marked the start of the Civil Rights movement." Despite their brave and defiant stand, when the women tried to enter the dining car they were turned away and had to buy their food from platform buffets: "I had heard about these things, but I was totally unprepared, coming from British Honduras, for this kind of behaviour. We thought this was not our country and we are not going to be part of these rules." When Nadia and her fellow travellers crossed the Mason Dixon Line from south into north, they noticed that the racial barriers on the train suddenly disappeared: "I remember we got to Washington and we crossed a river and the moment we got to the other side of that river all the barriers on the train came down. All the people moved and mixed and sat together and it was a totally different arrangement because we had crossed the Mason Dixon Line, and were now in the north and segregation was illegal."

After her initial training in Jamaica and the subsequent journey via America, Nadia arrived in England in June 1944: "There were only six of us when I journeyed to England on the *Queen Mary*, but the ship was also packed with thousands of American soldiers. I had no contact with American southerners. I was lucky! When our train arrived in London an air-raid siren went, and I was surprised that everyone strolled around so calm. I couldn't understand this. Then we were directed to an underground shelter. So, my first impression of London is the air-raid siren! I can't remember how long we stayed in London but we called our leave times 'home away from home' when we would stay with people who had come from our country of origin. I stayed with Mr Rupert Arthur and his family who were also from British Honduras. They lived in Benedict Road in Brixton. It was good to have contact with people from home. Shortly after our arrival we were sent to the ATS headquarters in Guildford in Surrey for basic training." Nadia turned down the opportunity to become a drill sergeant: "I was the only one who volunteered for the Royal Signals Corps in Edinburgh where I trained as a signals operator. We worked in shifts sending and receiving messages by Morse key and radio telephones. I was also a part-time physical training instructor with the ATS. In Edinburgh there was no racial tension. No problem at all. We had camaraderie." Nadia says she doesn't know why Scotland loomed so large in her mind: "I just knew I was heading for Scotland. I think it was because the colony and the settlement of British Honduras were peopled by Scottish British far more than by the English British, especially in the early days. Also, the British Honduran Forestry Unit was already in place in Scotland and I had an uncle, Carlton Fairweather, among them."

During the war, Nadia was aware of the appalling treatment of the segregated African American GIs who were based in Britain. She was also aware that some white American troops would verbally and physically assault black West Indians: "Quite often the white Americans mistook the black Caribbean people and attempted to treat them as they treated their own, and there was war on the streets of several of those northern cities because, especially the Jamaicans, they didn't think twice about putting the Americans in their place."

After the war, Nadia left the ATS and in 1946 went to teacher training college in Glasgow. After qualifying in 1949, she returned to British Honduras where she was headmistress of Galanjug Mission Infant School and lectured on infant education at Teachers' Training College and summer courses. “We were one of the families always involved in public affairs,” she recalled. “My father was a civil servant and, after his retirement, he entered politics and became Deputy Prime Minister of British Honduras. My mother was a schoolmistress. We became teachers, policemen, parsons, politicians. But I discovered I disliked what went with being a teacher there. I was expected to be a paragon of all the virtues and I couldn't accept that. When I tried to leave, and return to England, I was called unstable. The Director of Education there felt my duty lay with my people – a sort of ‘You will be the woman behind the man’ outlook. But I think you can contribute wherever you are in the world. Sometimes, if you go home, you contribute less. Any talent you have can shrivel up with restrictions.” Nadia returned to Britain in 1951.

In 2003, the Windrush Foundation honoured Nadia and many other organisations and individuals who had provided an outstanding service to Britain's black community. For their Lifetime Achievement Award for Contribution to the Arts, the Foundation selected Nadia for her distinguished career as an actress and folk singer.

Sources

Stephen Bourne, interviews with Nadia Cattouse, London, 8 August 1989 and 1 January 1997

Caroline Lang, *Keep Smiling Through: Women in the Second World War* (Cambridge University Press, 1989)

Ben Bousquet and Colin Douglas, *West Indian Women at War: British Racism in World War II* (Lawrence and Wishart, 1991)

16 Norma Best: The Best Experience

When Norma Leacock joined the Auxiliary Territorial Service (ATS) in British Honduras (now Belize) in 1944, she described herself as "one of those nice, middle-class black women seeking adventure." In 2010, when she was interviewed by a group of students from the Alexander Park Secondary School in Haringey for Patrick Vernon's documentary *Speaking Out and Standing Firm,* Norma explained: "I volunteered because I wanted to travel and we didn't have many opportunities to travel in those days. And that was the only opportunity so I thought I was going to have it. So, I applied and I was accepted." When the teenagers enquired about her army service and how she coped with racism, Norma replied: "Serving in the armed forces was wonderful. It was the best experience I've ever had. We were treated well. Our officers looked after us like our mothers. Every step I made in the army was fantastic. I didn't experience any racism because at that time all the people in England wanted to win the war, so colour didn't come into it. We were all fighting for the same thing, to win the war. The English people opened their homes to us, we were invited out for dinners, teas, no problems at all. But I think there were problems with the American forces, but it didn't hinder us."

Norma grew up in Belize City and Spanish Honduras and had, what she called, a lovely childhood: "It was a beautiful, perfect country. Safe. Our doors were open. It was a very *British* country." British Honduras was a colony, ruled by England, and its people were very loyal. Norma says: "Changes happened after the war but, when I was growing up, nobody questioned our loyalty to Britain, and there was no resentment of the British." Norma enjoyed school and dreamed of adventure: "I used to sit in school and just dream. We had to study the geography of England and I dreamed of these places. I thought I would love to go there."

Norma did not believe she would ever get to England, and at home she wanted to become an actress, but there were no opportunities for this dream. In fact, Norma discovered that her only career choices were the civil service, nursing, working in a store, or joining her family in education. She chose the latter and began work in a school. The war changed everything and enabled Norma to fulfil her dreams: "I was looking for adventure. I had always wanted to travel as a little girl, and this was the opportunity. A few of my relatives and friends said that London was cold and that I might not be able to withstand the weather, but I was determined to go."

Norma seized the opportunity to "see the world and do my service for dear old England. That was very important to me and for my family. We were very loyal people. Also, my father had served in the trenches in the First World War." Norma's father had served in Egypt, having joined the army at the same age as Norma, but she hadn't known about this until she told him of her plans to join the ATS. He told his daughter to "go for it" while her grandmother called her a "crazy girl."

In June 1944 Norma left home for Jamaica to become acclimatised "because Jamaica had a base in the mountains which were cold and England was cold. I reported to Kingston six weeks later and then travelled to New Orleans. The British were well in command. They were aware of the racial segregation that existed in America and they made sure we were treated well. They were nice to us in the hotel where we stayed, and we were taken on sight-seeing trips. The same thing happened in New York. People were curious when they saw us in uniform and wanted to know where we came from."

Norma arrived in Scotland in August 1944 and then took a train to London where she could do some sightseeing before going to Guildford for six weeks training. On her arrival, she discovered that she knew more about Britain than some of the British. She put that down to her very English education. She was also surprised by the accents: "I thought everyone would speak proper English! I was stunned when I heard the Scottish accent, or the Cockney accent." In 2010 she told the students from Alexander Park Secondary School: "The training was tough but we did it. We used to get up to mischief. Sometimes we used to take it in turns to hide, not go on parade, because we used to wear shorts for sports in the snow. But it was all done with love."

Norma's ambition was to be a driver, as her father had been during the First World War, but she could not cope with the weather. Instead she undertook administrative work, serving in Preston and later Derby. Norma remembers the discipline of the ATS: "You had to be in at certain times. You had to do certain jobs at certain times and when you went out you had to be on your best behaviour because you're wearing that uniform and whatever you do will reflect on others. The training I received strengthened me in character. But what was in me remained there."

In London Norma socialised with her colleagues: "We had a centre in Piccadilly, the Nuffield Centre, where *all* personnel from all different ranks met. Everybody just got on together. We were just wearing different uniforms. We were all friends." Norma was in London in May 1945 for VE Day and took part in the end of war celebrations on the Embankment. She later reflected: "I think the spirit of the war was that we were all fighting to win. All we could think about is to get in there, do a good job, let's get it over and done with. Colour didn't come into it."

After serving three years in the ATS from 1944 to 1947, Norma undertook a two-year college course. She studied to become a primary school teacher at Durham University and then returned home to British Honduras where, in 1951, she met Chief Petty Officer R. Best. They were married in 1954 and, at the end of his military service, they settled in Britain and raised a family. Norma worked as a teacher and headmistress from 1961 until her retirement in 1988.

Sources

Birthrights: Reunion, BBC2, 5 July 1993

Angelina Osborne and Arthur Torrington, *We Served: The Untold Story of the West Indian Contribution to World War II* (Krik Krak, 2005)

Norma Best, interviewed by Toby Brooks for the Imperial War Museum, 11 October 2007. Reference 30492.

17 Connie Mark: A Formidable Force

When the fiftieth anniversary of the outbreak of war was commemorated in 1989, Connie Mark, a former member of the ATS (Auxiliary Territorial Service) in Jamaica, was hurt that the contribution of West Indians, especially women, was ignored. When she was interviewed by Jacqui Harper in BBC television's *Hear-Say* in 1990, she said that she had a "bee in my bonnet" about this absence, because "every time I mentioned that I had been in the army, people would say they didn't know there were any black people in the war." During the planning of an Age Concern exhibition to commemorate the anniversary, Connie took along some photographs of West Indian ex-servicewomen: "That caused such a stir. People said: 'We never knew there were black ex-servicewomen', and that we even came to England. They are still ignorant." When Connie applied to the Greater London Arts, they gave her a grant and, in addition to finding some photographs in the Imperial War Museum, she borrowed a few from ex-servicewomen from across the West Indies. Connie put together an exhibition for the fiftieth anniversary celebrations and when asked by Jacqui Harper what the reaction was, Connie replied: "Shock. But I'm very glad that I stood my ground and I've done it and if I die tomorrow I have achieved what I wanted to have done."

Connie was born Constance MacDonald in Rollington Town, Kingston, Jamaica in 1923 and she saw herself as British, and patriotic: "England was our mother country. We were brought up to respect the Royal Family. I used to collect pictures of Princess Margaret and Princess Elizabeth. I adored them." When World War II was declared in 1939, Connie said that there was "a mood of fear in Jamaica". She said the English "put the fear of God in us. We were definitely positively told that the Germans wanted us because we were a stepping stone to the coast of America. So, we were on our tenterhooks all the time. Like England, Jamaica is an island. We depended on boats bringing things in. If you are short of oil because the boat coming in was torpedoed, then the whole bloody island has no oil." Connie also remembered the English officers who would "go into all the little corners of Jamaica and they would beg, literally beg you to come and fight for England because we were brought up that England was our mother country and obviously when your mother has problems, you've got to come and help her." Connie said that most of the Jamaican men who were recruited came from the countryside, and they had never left home. It came as a shock when they found themselves packed four to a bunk on a troop ship: "It was like pushing animals together because they really had the ships all cramped to make sure they get as many as they could to fight for England."

The reality of the war hit home to Connie early on when she found out that her best friend had been killed: "The first time the reality of war came to me was when I read in our local paper *The Gleaner* that Enid Edwards, from Port Antonio, died in a ship returning to Jamaica. The ship was torpedoed by the Germans. She was my best friend and we went to the same piano teacher. Enid studied at the Royal College of Music in London and passed all her exams with distinction. We were so proud of her and looked forward so much to her return to Jamaica. I cried for weeks."

Connie was made aware of the dangers that surrounded Jamaica and the other islands of the Caribbean. Ships were vulnerable to being torpedoed by the German U-Boats which is an abbreviation of Unterseeboot or undersea boat, a submarine that patrolled the Caribbean seas: "Guyana had a lot of gold and the Germans wanted to get it, and they also wanted oil from Trinidad, so there was a lot of submarines watching the island. It was very frightening." Connie remembered the air raid wardens who went around the towns and villages in Jamaica: "if by chance you had a speck of light showing from your house, you'd be arrested and fined."

Connie was just nineteen years old in 1943 when she joined the British army in Jamaica. Unlike other women from the Caribbean islands who joined up, Connie served her time in Jamaica: "I was going to take my exams in bookkeeping when my teacher came and said that they needed an expert and she said I was the best person." Connie was taken by the teacher to Up Park Camp, which was the military headquarters on South Camp Road in Kingston. Connie served in the ATS, the women's branch of the British army, for ten years. She worked as a Medical Secretary at the British Military Hospital in Kingston. Her duties included typing up the medical reports of those who had been injured in battle. Connie found herself documenting the terrible injuries men had sustained in bombings and combat. If Jamaicans wanted to find out if any of their loved ones were missing or had been killed in action, they went to Kingston Town: "At a place they call Parade there were two lists – a list of men reported missing and a list of men reported dead. And that list would go on and on – sometimes you'd go and you'd see the name of your cousin; you'd go back a few days later and see your friend's brother reported dead."

At Up Park Camp there was a prisoner of war camp and when war was declared all the German and Italian seamen working on merchant ships in the area were taken off and taken to the camp: "I worked at the hospital, and if they were sick they had to come up there for treatment. And we had a special corps that guarded them. The Germans and Italians have a lot of talent, so they used to make a lot of leather goods, and maybe twice a year they'd sell their wares that they made. And I remember I bought a lovely leather writing case. We used to buy things that they made. And another man was very proficient: he made doll's furniture. He must have been a carpenter or something in Germany. I remember I bought a whole drawing room and bedroom suite for my niece made by the German internee."

Connie remembered the fights that broke out, especially when the Irish Fusiliers arrived in Jamaica: "They all got drunk and they used to fight!" she said. "They fought the Jamaicans they met in bars. And of course, when they're coming to go to camp the Jamaicans waylaid them. So sometimes a whole road had to be put out of bounds because of fighting white soldiers. And we had the Brockville Rifles from Canada. And they could fight! They were always fighting! But a lot of it was prejudices, you see. They are white and they come to Jamaica and they just couldn't handle it. They just felt that they was kings, that, 'I can do anything and go anywhere.' And of course, Jamaican soldiers – no, not necessarily soldiers but Jamaicans whether soldiers or not – took exceptions to it. So, they started some nice good fight. Fortunately, with the Americans it wasn't so bad because the Americans wasn't in Kingston. They were in St Catherine, in another parish. Their base was actually in a place called Sandy Gully. We did not have that much to do with them. But everyone wanted to go and work on the American base because the pay was good."

Food shortages were common throughout the war: "We were short of things; I remember once we were short of rice, and asking a Jamaican not to eat rice and peas on a Sunday is a crime! And I remember once we were running very, very short. Everyone loves rice in Jamaica, most people. And a ship that was coming was torpedoed near Guyana. And instead of having rice we were having spaghetti and things like that. And oil! We haven't got oil in Jamaica, and if a ship was torpedoed that's it, we wouldn't have any oil."

Eventually Connie rose to the rank of Corporal: "It was quite an achievement to even reach the rank of Corporal. When you are a Lance Corporal, army regulations state that once one is promoted to Corporal you are entitled to tuppence per day. I applied for my tuppence a day and was

A group of servicemen and women who took part in West Indian Christmas Party, a 1944 BBC radio broadcast.

Left to right: Lt. Paul Miller (Jamaica), Pte L. St Prix (St Lucia), Pte Agnes Smith (British Guiana), F/Lt Osmund Kelsick DFC (Montserrat), Pte Doreen Hatt (Trinidad), F/O Ronald Hall (British Guiana), ACW Pearl Harry (Jamaica), Sgt. Vernon Lindo, RAF (Jamaica) and F/Lt Ulric Cross (Trinidad). Courtesy of the BBC

turned down by the War Office. When I asked why, I was told the Jamaican ATS were not entitled to this. I was in a British regiment attached to the Royal Army Medical Corps but I was still not entitled. That was my first experience of racial discrimination. The Queen still owes me eight years of tuppence a day! That may not sound a lot now, but in those days, it added up. So, I have had my little prejudices thrown at me."

Connie remembered VE Day as a marvellous time: "everybody was happy 'cause as far as we were concerned, the war was finished. Everybody was happy. Everybody just jumped up and down; the war was over, and it meant that no more of our people would be killed. We had parties, and everybody took it as an excuse to have a party, a drink up, and get stone-blind drunk. I didn't used to drink in those days; I just went to all the parties that there were. Yeah, you were glad that the war was over, and people weren't going to die. You didn't have troop ships coming in with people sick, or blinded, or with missing limbs."

When the war ended, Connie's commander put her up for the British Empire Medal (BEM), but she did not receive it. She believed she was overlooked because she refused to clean the houses of the English ATS officers. However, in 1992, she did finally receive the BEM, nearly forty years after she had left Jamaica and settled in London. When Connie arrived in London in 1954 she said:

there were very few people who didn't have a story of having lost someone or knew someone who lost someone, or telling you of streets that had been bombed...the war was still very much part of what was happening in Britain, and people were living in prefabs, and that was quite strange. You couldn't understand why they were living in what we saw as huts. I get very annoyed that people don't want to accept and remain ignorant of the fact of how the West Indies were involved in the war and how we were brought up to love the King, love the Queen, to love England and to respect England. Then when you come here after the war, what do you see? You see a sign saying 'No Blacks, no Irish, no dogs, no children'. That hurt, that really used to hurt.

When Connie joined the West Indian ex-Servicemen's Association she raised the profile of the contribution women had made to the British war effort, and persuaded the organisation to extend its name to the West Indian ex-Servicemen and Women's Association. Health permitting, she regularly marched in the annual Remembrance Day parade at the Cenotaph. Inspired by the Jamaican doctress, Mary Seacole, a heroine of the Crimean war, Connie was instrumental in founding the Friends of Mary Seacole organisation, which has since become the Mary Seacole Memorial Association. In 2001 Connie was awarded the MBE.

When Connie died in 2007, her obituarist, Margaret Busby, described her as a champion of Caribbean culture and "a formidable force within the black community. She was much in demand for her poetry and storytelling events, using oral history to address the young." In 2008, Connie was posthumously honoured with a blue plaque by the Nubian Jak Community Trust, in association with Care UK and Hammersmith and Fulham Council. It was unveiled at Connie's former home, Mary Seacole House, in Invermead Close, Hammersmith.

Connie Mark died in London on 3 June 2007 at the age of 83.

Sources

The Motherland Calls: African Caribbean Experiences (Hammersmith and Fulham Ethnic Communities Oral History Project, 1989)

Ben Bousquet and Colin Douglas, *West Indian Women at War* (Lawrence and Wishart, 1991)

Angelina Osborne and Arthur Torrington, *We Served: The Untold Story of the West Indian Contribution to World War II* (Krik Krak, 2005)

Margaret Busby, 'Connie Mark' (obituary), *The Guardian* (16 June 2007)

Expatriates Part 3

18 Adelaide Hall Carries On…and Goes to Germany

The BBC loved Adelaide Hall and, during the war, she became a regular fixture at BBC Broadcasting House. The BBC contracted her on many occasions for guest appearances in music and variety radio broadcasts. Such was her popularity with listeners, in 1941 the BBC presented Adelaide in her own series, *Piccadixie*. The *Radio Times* described the secret of her popularity: "good nature and love of life. There is a tremendous warmth of feeling in Adelaide, a great goodwill towards everybody. She loves singing, she loves broadcasting, she loves humanity. More than anything, she loves making people happy. She's always smiling, cheerful, and genuinely pleased to see you, always ready for a joke, a song, a party – anything. She's absurdly generous, and will do anything for anybody, as is shown by the large amount of work she does for charity. She has a great eye for colour, can't resist a brilliant frock and gay, rather flamboyant jewellery…She knits brightly coloured jerseys for the troops." When the BBC engaged her for another series in 1943, called *Wrapped in Velvet*, the *Radio Times* enthused: "Whenever you see Adelaide she is smiling that shining smile and looking, with her outsize finger-rings, gay as a parakeet. She is a charming, laughing woman who, with a voice like that, just couldn't help being a charming, laughing star."

In 1943 Adelaide received an invitation from Britain's top showman, the theatrical manager and impresario Charles B. Cochran, to take part in *Seventy Years of Song*, an all-star gala at the Royal Albert Hall on 16 June. This was in aid of TocH, which created new clubs worldwide for men and women of the United Nations Forces. King George VI and Queen Elizabeth, as well as various political and diplomatic figures, attended the spectacular event, described as 'a costume cavalcade of tunes heard in music halls and concert halls from 1870 to the present'. Adelaide took part in the second half and sang 'I'm a Little Blackbird, Looking for a Bluebird', the song popularised by the 1920s African American star Florence Mills at the London Pavilion in C. B. Cohran's *Blackbirds* revue. Other stars featured in the second half included the cream of British show business including 'Hutch', Evelyn Laye, Mary Ellis, Noel Coward and Vera Lynn.

When Adelaide joined the Entertainments National Service Association (ENSA), one of the first things she did was to have a uniform specially tailored for her by Madame Adele of Grosvenor Street. She said: "Oh, it was smart! It was sand brown, with a lovely cap, and I had a shirt and tie too. It was a first-class uniform but I couldn't stand the collar. It was very stiff." Adelaide loved the uniform, and wore it with pride whenever and wherever she could. She told her husband Bert, "If you could be in the Merchant Navy, I'm going to be a soldier!" Adelaide was proud of the fact that she was one of the first entertainers to enter Germany before the war was over. She recalled travelling to Germany on a 'plane full of officers, and being the only woman present in uniform. She said: "I travelled through Germany for ENSA, appearing in garrison theatres everywhere. As the war began to end, I moved along with the troops and it was a very dangerous thing to do, but I didn't think about that. I just did what I had to do. I was on edge, and sometimes very frightened, but I persevered. It was hard work but I'm glad I went. I loved it. We went through Hamburg, Hanover, Dusseldorf, Celle, Frankfurt, Munich, Bordenhause and Wolfenbüttel. Eventually we got to Berlin, and then we came all the way back!"

ENSA provided Adelaide with her own jeep and a driver: "We arrived at the camp and the hall would be packed with soldiers. The door opened and the place was full of soldiers and smoke. I did my cabaret act and the boys had a ball. Sometimes we didn't have a stage so we had to improvise from the floor. At some of the concerts I sang to thousands of soldiers and it was so moving when they joined in."

When Victory in Europe Day (VE Day) was announced on 8 May 1945, Adelaide was in Hamburg in the middle of her tour. She then became one of the first entertainers to arrive in Berlin to congratulate the troops after the city had been liberated. She said: "In the towns and cities we visited there was not a street in sight – nothing. They had all been razed to the ground, and people were putting up little boards, made from bits of wood, to identify the names of the streets that used to be there." After the war Bert couldn't get her out of the uniform made by Madame Adele. He told his wife: "The war is over now, honey, you can let that uniform go!"

In a letter to the author of this book, Mrs Jean Brown, who had served as a Corporal in the Women's Auxiliary Air Force during World War II, recalled seeing Adelaide at the Empire Theatre in Newcastle-on-Tyne in 1944: "I was serving in the WAAF and stationed in Newcastle, Adelaide was the star of the show at the Empire Theatre. About six of us were invited to sell programmes at the theatre. Some of the proceeds was for the RAF Benevolent Fund. After a marvellous show, we were asked to go and meet her in the dressing-room. I have never forgotten her, quite a large lady with a beautiful smile. She was wearing a lilac satin evening dress and it was off the shoulder style. She was also wearing lovely earrings which were shaped like small hands and each had a brilliant red stone. I'm thinking rubies and they probably were, but I still have a vivid picture in my memory. She was very sincere and interested in what we were all doing and how we were coping so far from home. I am sorry I've lost my programme as I am sure we could get her autograph. It gives me great pleasure to tell you that I met this wonderful star whose voice could have lifted the roof off!"

In Chapter 28, 'Adelaide Hall: Adopted Daughter of London', Adelaide has made London her permanent home.

19 Elisabeth Welch Goes to Gibraltar

In November 1942 Elisabeth Welch was appearing in Manchester when she received a telegram from the War Office asking if she would travel to Gibraltar. Thousands of troops were stationed there but had been provided with very little entertainment. Only a revue called *Swingtime Follies* and one other ENSA show had visited Gibraltar. Elisabeth was invited to join a first-rate entertainment called *Christmas Party* with great artists of the theatre, like Edith Evans and John Gielgud, and the popular comedienne Beatrice Lillie. The company flew out to Gibraltar in December 1942 and returned to England in January 1943. Elisabeth later recalled:

Well, what greater compliment could be asked of a foreigner than to join the company of people like Edith Evans, Beatrice Lillie, John Gielgud and Michael Wilding? I was very proud, and grateful! We were asked by the War Office to go out to Gibraltar to entertain the troops. Not ENSA, but HM Government itself, the men with red braid on their caps. I felt very grand. We flew out in a Dutch plane with the windows all blacked out because we weren't supposed to see where we were going. We landed in Lisbon in what looked like a sea of swastikas. Because Portugal was neutral everyone stopped there for repairs and refuelling, and it was quite a shock to step out of the plane and see Nazi planes all round us. We girls gave our own brass hats a shock too. We were all three wearing trousers and they asked us frostily to change, which we did not.

Christmas Party was organized by Hugh 'Binkie' Beaumont of H. M. Tennant's, a management that made sure its stars played troop shows. Said Elisabeth: "We began rehearsing for the first show, and John Gielgud had been given a poem to read. It was a tribute to the men who were fighting for us and John got into a funk about it. He's a shy man, and he said, 'How can I go out and recite something about fighting for our country when we're not in uniform and we'll be flown back to London and looked after and lauded? How can I stand in front of these men?' I told John, don't worry, I'd sing something to set the scene. So I began to sing Noel Coward's 'London Pride' quietly behind the curtains to get the boys into the mood. Then he spoke these words, and you could hear a pin drop. They were very emotional days, especially out there in Gibraltar where the boys were going to be killed and the ships to be sunk. It's hard to sing when your throat tightens up and you are fighting back tears, but for an actor it's different, and John has always had a little nervy thing, an emotional sort of timbre to his voice."

During their four-week stay in Gibraltar, the company performed fifty-six shows, including one on board ship to more than 2,000 men, two in the local hospitals, and some on board battleships and aircraft carriers. They also toured gun-sites where they talked to the men. Most of the shows were given in the island's Rock Theatre which held about 750 people and it was packed at every performance, officers and men all sitting together, which created a better atmosphere than in the English camps where they were always separated. Most of the troops had been stationed in Gibraltar for two years and having a very dull time, so they were a responsive and grateful audience. There were two performances every night, including Sundays. When Elisabeth took to the stage, she was at the height of her powers as an artist, briefly described by John Gielgud in the May 1943 edition of *Theatre Arts:* "Elisabeth Welch sings 'Prayer for Rain', 'Begin the Beguine', and 'Solomon', in a black dress against a white satin curtain, and you can hear a pin drop while she is singing, but when she has finished the thunder of applause can be heard in the street." In Chapter 29, 'Elisabeth Welch: At Home Abroad', Elisabeth visits her beloved Paris after the war, and then makes a triumphant appearance in post-war London in a critically acclaimed revue.

Josephine Baker celebrates VE (Victory in Europe) Day with a broadcast for the BBC (1945)

Credit: BBC

20 Josephine Baker: Rainbow Warrior

From humble beginnings in the slums of St Louis to a jet-set career as an internationally acclaimed entertainer, Josephine Baker was always much more than an exotic cabaret star. She symbolised a new freedom for women in the 1920s and 1930s. As an active member of the French resistance during World War II, she was decorated by the French government for her contribution to fighting Hitler and fascism.

Josephine was born in the heart of the ghetto of St Louis, Missouri in 1906. By the early 1920s she was working as a chorus girl. Hungry for fame, she got the break she wanted in 1925 when she journeyed to Paris as one of the stars of *La Revue Negre*, an all-black cast revue. Josephine was a sensation. She made her entrance entirely nude, except a few feathers here and there, and news of her triumphant Paris debut swept through Europe. Overnight the runaway from St Louis became the toast of Paris. A year or so later she dazzled Paris again in a show at the famous Folies Bergere. Leaping onto the stage wearing nothing but bananas and a smile, she captivated her audience.

Those who were enthralled by her on-stage extravagance were anxious to find out if the real-life Josephine was just as exciting. She understood this and helped to spread stories about her lavish lifestyle. On one occasion she was recognised in the Champs-Elysees holding onto the leashes of two pet leopards and, within two years of her Paris debut, Josephine was said to have received 46,000 fan letters; 40,000 love letters; and 1,192 marriage proposals. During the late 1920s and early 1930s Josephine exploited the French and European view of the black woman as a savage and an exotic, but gradually she succeeded in constructing an elaborate image of herself as one of the world's most glamorous and exciting women. In this respect, black women, apart from those in the conservative middle-classes in America, took pleasure in reading about her European exploits. For urban African Americans, she was a heroine.

After the outbreak of World War II, Josephine continued to work as an entertainer and she was always popular with the troops. In the summer of 1940, when France fell to the Germans, Josephine left Paris before the occupation and went to the Chateau des Milandes, her home in the south of France. It was here that she

'Josephine Baker Gives Soldiers a Victory Song', *Picture Post* (2 June 1945)

He Hasn't Looked That Way Since He Was Six. "Silly, Isn't it?" Says Miss Baker
She's just brought him on to the stage, and he's shy. Why he's shy, we don't know. Is it because he's on the stage? Or because Miss Baker's holding his arm? We couldn't say. All we know is that if we were in his boots, we'd be shy too.

Josephine Baker Gives Soldiers a Victory Song

But She Soon Shows the Troops How
The first thing you've got to learn if you want everything's easy.

12

What She's Singing

I have two loves, my country and Paris;
My heart is divided between them.
My Savannah is lovely, but—why deny it?
Everything about Paris bewitches me.

J'ai deux amours, mon pays et Paris,
Par eux toujours, mon coeur est ravi.
Ma Savanne est belle, mais à quoi bon le nier?
Ce qui m'ensorcèle, c'est Paris tout entier.

to Do Their Stuff: "Just Relax," says Miss Baker
to dance like Miss Baker is to let yourself go. After that, The troops are willing to learn.

She Finds New Talent; He Resists. "Aw, C'mon!" Says Miss Baker.
His friend explains that you can't refuse a lady. That's all right, he thinks,—for the other chaps. Miss Baker pulls; he pulls; Miss Baker wins.

13

Credit: Getty

gave refuge to the Free French led by Charles de Gaulle and provided them with visas. Josephine also hid members of the resistance movement in her chateau. Early in the war, Josephine was recruited by the French military intelligence. As an undercover agent for the resistance, Josephine collected what information she could about German troop locations from officials and diplomats she socialised with at parties. Their conversations were centred almost entirely on wartime activities and they were often careless about being overheard by Josephine who, to them, was just an entertainer. Her fame enabled her to rub shoulders with high-ranking Japanese officials and Italian bureaucrats, and to report to England what she had heard without raising suspicion. The risks that she took as an undercover agent have never fully come to light, but the detailed notes that she wrote in invisible ink on the pages of her sheet music could easily have cost her her life.

Josephine was awarded the honorary rank of lieutenant in the Free French Air Force for raising money for the French war effort. After the war, the French government decorated her for her wartime bravery and activities with three of their highest awards: Legion d'Honneur, Croix de Guerre and the Rosette de la Resistance. When Paris was liberated on 25 August 1944, Josephine returned to France with the Free French Forces. She re-entered the city of her dreams wearing her blue Air Auxiliary uniform complete with gold epaulets. Josephine was so proud of her uniform that she would occasionally wear it until the end of her life. She then made many concert appearances all over France for army posts and hospitals, putting herself in debt by refusing payment for her services.

Josephine was known in Britain, but by the start of World War II she had only made a handful of professional appearances here, including a four-week engagement in a revue at London's Prince Edward Theatre in 1933. However, on 2 May 1943, Basil Dean, the Director of the British Entertainments National Service Association (ENSA), invited her to join his organisation. Said her biographer Patrick O'Connor in *Josephine Baker* (1988): "He appointed one of his personal assistants, Harry Hurford-Janes, to look after her. Hurford-Janes became one of Josephine's closest and staunchest friends from then until her death. He recalled: 'I was detailed to safeguard Miss Baker's feelings following certain indignities of race or class for which the British, American or Egyptian authorities were responsible.'" O'Connor added that Josephine and Hurford-Janes took part in many different activities for ENSA and quoted a letter from Hurford-Janes to Josephine which he had written to the star in 1949: "One of my most cherished memories is that night we dragged a little piano into the ward of a Canadian hospital and you sang 'I'll Be Seeing You' until you were so tired you nearly dropped. How even the nurses stood with tears in their eyes and those poor helpless men – many of whom would never recover - lying on their backs unable to move, only their eyes showing the relief and comfort you brought them." Hurford-Janes always signed his letters to Josephine 'Your affectionate brother' and after her death he just remembered her as 'that dear mystic, magical, unpredictable, idealistic, foolish, generous and warm woman.'

Josephine returned to London at the end of the war to take part in a victory show at the Adelphi Theatre in the Strand on 29 April 1945. This had been organised for the forces by the *News of the World* newspaper. Josephine was still in London a week later, on 8 May, celebrating Victory in Europe Day (VE Day). She made a radio broadcast for the BBC in *Break for Music*, described as an "ENSA show for war-workers" and she was the guest artist in an edition of BBC radio's popular *Music-Hall* series. Then there was a personal appearance on stage at London's Cambridge Theatre on 14 May with Noel Coward in a Gala Variety Concert.

When Josephine came back to Britain in 1948 she guest-starred on BBC television in two cabaret shows *Café Continental*, in which her songs included 'Weekend in Havana' and 'La Petite Tonkinoise' and *The Josephine Baker Show*, in which she sang Edith Piaf's 'La Vie en Rose' and her own 'theme song', 'J'ai Deux Amours'. Josephine continued to work as an entertainer until the end of her life. She also found time to campaign for civil rights, and adopt twelve children of different nationalities. She called them her 'Rainbow Tribe'.

Josephine was never forgotten in Britain. In spite of her busy life, she occasionally found time to return for cabaret appearances. The year before she died, Josephine took part in the 1974 Royal Variety Performance at the London Palladium and made a guest appearance in BBC television's *The Good Old Days*. In 1986 British television paid tribute to the legend with Channel 4's BAFTA-nominated documentary *Chasing a Rainbow*.

Josephine Baker died in Paris on 12 April 1975 at the age of 68.

Sources

Stephen Bourne, 'Rainbow Warrior', *The Voice* (18 January 1986)

Bryan Hammond and Patrick O'Connor, *Josephine Bake*r (Jonathan Cape, 1988)

Britain Part 3

Ida Shepley

21 At Home with Amanda Ira Aldridge

In August 1945, the singing teacher Amanda Ira Aldridge, then aged seventy-nine, moved into the home of one of her pupils, Ida Shepley. Amanda had not been happy living in Henley-on-Thames, and she was overjoyed when Ida and her husband Charles offered her rooms in their home in Chiswick. Amanda kept her grand piano in Ida and Charles's drawing room and acquired Ida's small piano in her upstairs flat. When she wrote to her friend Margarita Downing in New York that same month, Amanda exclaimed "Behold my new address! Yes, I am back in London – and oh! So glad. One of my pupils, my very dear Ida Shepley, and her husband have bought this home and offered me the top flat – (at a rental that I can afford). I moved in on Friday and am very happy and comfortable. All my own furniture and belongings around me."

Amanda was excited by the prospect of living in Chiswick, but she was also saddened by the destruction caused by air raids in the area. She informed Margarita: "The neighbourhood is very healthy and within easy bus ride from Oxford Circus...All around – this area has been terribly bombed, but fortunately this home escaped with shattered windows and a certain amount of damage which has all been repaired – and so I hope Providence will be kind and let me live to enjoy this peace."

Irish-born Margarita Downing had been married to the African American journalist and dramatist Henry Downing. They had settled in London in 1895 and remained there until they returned to America in 1917. In London the Downings had befriended several members of the small black middle-class community in Edwardian England including Amanda and her family, as well as the mixed-race composer Samuel Coleridge-Taylor. Known as 'The Black Mahler' or 'The Hiawatha Man' (after his most famous composition), Samuel died young, in 1912, at the age of thirty-seven. However, Samuel's daughter, Avril, born in 1903, then followed in her father's footsteps and became a composer and conductor. Henry Downing died in Harlem Hospital in 1928 and Margarita, who lived in New York corresponded with her friend Amanda into the 1940s.

When Amanda wrote the 'Chiswick' letter to Margarita, she had enjoyed a long and successful career as one of Britain's most respected composers at a time when few women were successful in establishing themselves in the male-dominated profession. In later years, she turned her attention to being a voice teacher. Amanda's background was distinguished for when she was

Ida Shepley and Neville Crabbe in a rehearsal for *Something Different* for the Negro Theatre Company (1948)

born in south London in 1866, her father, Ira Aldridge, was one of the most celebrated actors of the Victorian era. Tragically, Amanda never knew him for he died while touring Poland in 1867, only seventeen months after Amanda was born at the Aldridge family's home, Luranah Villa, in Penge. In honour of her father, Amanda added the name Ira to her own.

Ira was a celebrated African American tragedian. He made his first London appearance in 1825 at the Coburg Theatre, now the Old Vic in Waterloo Road where his portrait is now displayed. After their father's death, all three Aldridge children showed great musical promise and their Swedish-born mother, Paulina, encouraged this. Amanda later said that her mother strongly encouraged her work as a composer: "She never wearied of trying to induce me to write down the melodies that I sometimes hummed or played. I also feel that my mother influenced the development of the African side of me by her veneration and pride in the memory of our father Ira Aldridge."

One of Amanda's earliest concerts took place at Crystal Palace in 1881 when she was just fifteen years old. Two years later, at the age of seventeen, she won a foundation scholarship to the newly opened Royal College of Music where she studied piano and had singing lessons with Jenny Lind, a famous opera singer who was known as the Swedish Nightingale. Sadly, Amanda's singing career ended after an attack of laryngitis damaged her throat, but she remembered what Jenny Lind had said to her: "Never mind what happens to your throat. You can always earn a livelihood as a singing teacher, because you have a good insight into voice theory and practice."

As a voice teacher, her many students in London included the young Paul Robeson who she helped to prepare for his first appearance as Shakespeare's Othello in 1930. Two other distinguished African American pupils who visited her at her London studio were the tenor Roland Hayes and contralto Marian Anderson. When Amanda settled in Chiswick in 1945, she continued to travel to Weeks Studio in Hanover Square, Westminster, where she taught singing and diction for several hours a day. When questioned about the possibility of retirement, Amanda replied: "Life without music would be unbearable. I cannot keep still."

It was in the 1930s that Amanda befriended Ida Shepley who was one of her students and also mixed-race. Ida appreciated Amanda's teaching skills, and in 1938 she commenced her career as a much admired contralto. Ida was successful as a concert artist and vocalist on BBC radio. Amanda described Ida to her American friend Margarita as "partly West African and on her mother's side Canadian (white)" but this was not true, for Ida had been born in Cheshire in 1908 to an English mother and Trinidadian father. Little is known about Ida's early life. When she married Charles Skilbeck Smith in 1937 at the age of twenty-eight, she did not enter a profession on her marriage certificate. Ida began broadcasting on BBC radio in 1938 and for the next decade she made over seventy appearances in a wide range of music and variety shows. These included *Mississippi Nights, Brief Interlude* with Elisabeth Welch, *The Empire Sings, Negro Spirituals, A Victory Rhapsody, Variety Bandbox, Fantasia* and the series *Soft Lights and Sweet Music*. Harry Gold, a musician, who sometimes broadcast with Ida in the 1940s, remembered her as "a very good singer with a lovely, happy personality." Ida also made her first television appearances for the BBC in *See for Yourself* (1947) and *Black, Brown and Beige* (1948).

Amanda's coaching also helped Ida to make a successful transition to 'straight' acting when she appeared in two productions of Eugene O'Neill's *All God's Chillun' Got Wings* for the Colchester Repertory Theatre in 1944 and the left-wing Unity Repertory Company in 1946. In their review, *The Stage* newspaper commented that Ida "plays with a confident touch, obviously with complete psychological grasp of the part which she successfully projects." When *Theatre World* magazine reviewed the production, it described the Guyanese actor Robert Adams and Ida as "gifted guest artists" who gave "convincing performances as the negro who contracts a mixed marriage and his sister of the biased outlook." In spite of the lack of good roles for black actresses in Britain at this time, the success of *All God's Chillun'* helped Ida being cast in a couple of West End plays: *Caviar to the General* at the Whitehall Theatre in 1947 and *The Vigil* at the Embassy and Prince of Wales's Theatres in 1948. She also joined the Negro Repertory Company for a one-off theatrical event on 4 July 1948 called *Something Different* which utilized Ida's talents as an actress in a dramatic scene from Clifford Odets's *Golden Boy* and as a singer of spirituals.

In her 1945 letter to Margarita Downing, Amanda made a reference to Avril Coleridge-Taylor: "I met, by accident, Coleridge-Taylor's daughter. She recognised me. I would not have known her after so many years. She told me that her composition – a symphony – was to be played, under her conductorship, at Bournemouth. She was very charming and good-looking. I inquired after her mother and brother – both well. When I introduced my pupil, Ida Shepley, she expressed her great pleasure, for she had heard Ida sing one of her father's songs on the wireless, only a week or so ago and had written to Stanford Robinson (the conductor) asking him to thank her (Ida) for her beautiful rendering." The BBC radio programme featuring Ida and referred to by Amanda was *Sunday Rhapsody:*

Avril Coleridge-Taylor

The Music of Coleridge-Taylor, which was broadcast on the Home Service on 3 June 1945. By the 1940s, Avril had established herself in the music world with over ninety compositions, including *In Memoriam RAF* and as the conductor of the BBC Symphony Orchestra and the London Symphony Orchestra. She was the first woman to conduct the band of the Royal Marines. Amanda Ira Aldridge's relationships with her pupils, especially Ida Shepley, was often of a personal nature, possibly because, in later life, she had no remaining family of her own. Another student and friend was the actor Earl Cameron who arrived in London from Bermuda in 1939. When Earl decided to turn professional, he understood that he needed some help. He later recalled:

I had no training as an actor, but in 1947 my friend, Ida Shepley, introduced me to Miss Amanda Ira Aldridge, a singing teacher and composer who was prominent in the music world in England. Miss Aldridge was about eighty but still giving elocution lessons and instructing people in voice projection. She was light-skinned, rather short and stocky. She was a lovely, well-spoken, delicate and dignified lady with a tremendous sense of humour. She could laugh about most things. She was a courteous, beautiful human being, but not wealthy. I had the highest regard for her, and we got on extremely well. She helped me tremendously and I continued having lessons with her for at least two years. She told me about her father, and showed me pictures of him.

Amanda Ira Alridge died on the day before her 90th birthday in Coulsdon, Surrey, on 9 March 1956.

Ida Shepley died in Sydenham on 12 March 1975 at the age of 66.

Avril Coleridge-Taylor died in Seaford on the East Sussex coast on 21 December 1998 at the age of 95.

Sources

Ida Shepley, 'Amanda Ira Aldridge', *Checkers* Vol 1, No 5 (January 1949)

Edward Scobie, 'Amanda Ira Aldridge', *Flamingo* (March 1962)

Herbert Marshall and Mildred Stock, *Ira Aldridge: The Negro Tragedian* (Rockliff, 1958)

Harry Gold, interview with Stephen Bourne, London, 10 January 1994

Earl Cameron, interview with Stephen Bourne, London, 2 July 1997

Jeffrey *Green, Black Edwardians: Black People in Britain 1901-1914* (Frank Cass, 1998)

'Africa Speaks in Manchester', *Picture Post* (10 November 1945). One of the photos features Amy Ashwood Garvey on stage at the Manchester Pan-African Conference. Courtesy of Getty Images

22 Amy Ashwood Garvey and the 1945 Manchester Pan-African Congress

In the General Election of July 1945, the British people voted for something different and the Labour Party was elected to replace Winston Churchill's wartime Conservative-led coalition government. The British people hoped for a better future, with more job opportunities and improved health care. The latter was eventually provided with the launch of the National Health Service in 1948. After the war, black British citizens at home and across the Empire in the colonies also looked forward to an improved standard of living. They also saw the possibility of an end to colonial rule. During World War II, in addition to the long-established West African Students' Union and the League of Coloured Peoples, amongst others, many new black-led organisations had been formed in Britain.

In October 1945, the Fifth Pan-African Congress was held in Manchester and it was attended by representatives from many of Britain's black-led organisations as well as some from Africa, the Caribbean and the USA. The Congress called for self-government in the colonies, and demanded an end to racism, which was known as the 'colour bar' in Britain. Many of those who attended the Congress, such as Kwame Nkrumah of Ghana and Jomo Kenyatta of Kenya, went on to become leaders of these African countries when they were decolonised. There were 33 delegates from the West Indies and 35 from various British organisations. The presence of 77-year-old W. E. B. Du Bois, the highly respected African American scholar and civil rights activist, was historic. However, the British Press scarcely mentioned the conference apart from a photo spread in *Picture Post* (10 November 1945). Kwame Nkrumah, along with George Padmore, Ras T. Makonnen, Peter Abrahams and Amy Ashwood Garvey, were among those involved in organising the Congress. Amy Ashwood Garvey and a fellow Jamaican Alma La Badie were the only two women delegates who gave presentations. Amy Ashwood Garvey also chaired the opening session on 15 October.

Amy Ashwood Garvey was born in Jamaica in 1897 into a 'comfortable' family home and she became the first wife of the Jamaican nationalist leader Marcus Garvey. They were married in 1919 but she became a political activist in her own right. Her political activities were linked mainly with her work in the Universal Negro Improvement Association (UNIA), which had been founded by her husband. His teachings were primarily concerned with inspiring black people to see beauty in themselves, and emphasising African unity. Amy went to the USA in 1918 and played an important role in the UNIA branches there as Marcus Garvey's chief aide and secretary. After divorcing Garvey in 1922, Amy travelled extensively. She always took a keen interest in social welfare, politics and the cultural life in the many countries (including England) in which she lived. Amy remained a pan-Africanist and feminist until she died.

When Amy addressed the Manchester Pan-African Congress on 19 October 1945, she said: "Very much has been written and spoken of the Negro, but for some reason very little has been said about the black woman. She has been shunted into the social background to be a child-bearer. This has been principally her lot. In the island of Jamaica, we have two classes of women: the rich and the poor… [Middle-class women] take no active part whatever in the political development of the country. The very class from which we should derive inspiration remains indifferent. It is among the women teachers that we find a progressive movement. There are ten thousand black women in the schools of Jamaica…Because of the low standard of living, our people find it necessary to emigrate to various places, and our women have gone along with our men to Cuba, Panama and America."

Alma La Badie, representing the UNIA, was the only other female recorded in the proceedings. Alma came from a middle-class Jamaican family and had paid her own fare to Britain to serve in the Women's Auxiliary Air Force. She served in Britain from 1943 to 1947. During her time in Britain, she became involved with Pastor Daniels Ekarte's 'Brown Babies' home in Liverpool. These were the abandoned mixed-race children of white Englishwomen and African American GIs. At the Congress on 15 October Alma made an impassioned plea about the welfare of these children: "One of the most vital problems that the Congress is asked to consider is that of the children left behind by coloured American troops. Many of these babies were born to married women whose husbands were serving overseas. Now that the husbands were returning the condition of forgiveness was that the children be sent elsewhere. Consequently it was imperative to form a committee to look after these babies. There is a home actually in existence, but money is needed to help it to function. We cannot allow the children to suffer for the mistakes of their fathers and mothers." At the Congress on 19 October Alma elaborated on the problems faced by Jamaican women, connecting the "high illegitimate birth rate" to the fact that "women have little means of livelihood, and, therefore, get into difficulties."

F. R. Kankam-Boadu was one of the West African Students' Union delegates at the Congress. Fifty years later, when Marika Sherwood interviewed him for the book she co-authored with Hakim Adi, *The 1945 Manchester Pan-African Congress Revisited* (1995), he recalled the following: "a contingent of West Indian Royal Air Force girls, who were serving in the British Air Forces, more than graced the occasion and far from only forming a bodyguard for the lady in the chair, passionately indulged in the speeches of the day. A Miss La Badie I remember to have drawn tears from the audience, recounting vividly the miseries of sufferings of West Indian girls on the islands." He also recalled Amy Ashwood Garvey who had opened the meeting "with a very mature and balanced speech touching on freedom and humanity: soldiers of the Commonwealth and others had fought and sacrificed their lives to this end, and freedom and peace should be the prize to be won. She directed the audiences' mind to democracy as opposed to dictatorship, which had caused wars and miseries, and appealed for peace and fraternity among nations. She asked for freedom and self-rule for the British colonies. She referred to racial discrimination and other prejudices and advised their liquidation."

Amy Ashwood Garvey died in Kingston, Jamaica on 3 May 1969 at the age of 72.

Alma La Badie died in Islington, London in 1985 at the age of 76.

Sources

Peter Fryer, *Staying Power: The History of Black People in Britain* (Pluto Press, 1984)

Hakim Adi, *The History of the African and Caribbean Communities in Britain* (Wayland, 1995)

Hakim Adi and Marika Sherwood, *The 1945 Manchester Pan-African Congress Revisited* (New Beacon Books, 1995)

'Historic Figures', *Black and Asian Studies Association*, No. 16 (September 1996)

23 Television is Here Again

In the pre-war years of the BBC's television service (1936-39), before World War II interrupted the service, black artists made important contributions to entertainment programmes. Some of these were inspired by various black cabaret shows then popular in London's West End and the programmes featured glamorous stars like Nina Mae McKinney, Valaida Snow and Elisabeth Welch. In *Harlem in Mayfair* (1939), Adelaide Hall broadcast in a live transmission from her popular West End nightclub, but these shows only reached a small, exclusive audience. In those days, all television programmes were transmitted live, usually from the BBC studios at Alexandra Palace, to a limited audience who were exclusively white and middle-class because television was an expensive commodity, costing the same as a new car. Between 1936 and 1949, television could only reach London. However, the pre-war BBC television service was short-lived and ended on 1 September 1939. On that day Germany invaded Poland and the government gave BBC executives exactly ten minutes notice to shut down. The screen simply went blank during a Mickey Mouse cartoon. There was no announcement. Concerns had been expressed that the signal from the mast at Alexandra Palace would attract enemy aircraft. On 3 September war was declared.

BBC television was officially relaunched at Alexandra Palace on 7 June 1946. To promote the new service, the BBC produced a documentary film called *Television is Here Again*. It featured a host of television announcers and stars from the entertainment world including Elisabeth Welch who sang 'St Louis Blues' and 'Stormy Weather' accompanied by Debroy Somers and his Orchestra. The film celebrated the post-war resumption of the BBC's television service and it was partly used to demonstrate the medium to potential viewers when they considered purchasing television sets. It was first shown on BBC television on 17 June 1946 and as a support feature in cinemas.

On 24 June 1946, the Trinidadian folk singer Edric Connor introduced Ballets Negres, Britain's first black dance company, to British television audiences. Its founder was the Jamaican Berto Pasuka. They made their debut at the Twentieth Century Theatre in London's Westbourne Grove in April 1946 and in the *Evening Standard,* the critic Caryl Brahms enthused: "A new kind of ballet was born last night…I am confident that wherever the Ballet Negres may go, rhythm raised at times to a frenzy, bright in colour, and strong in sound, will prove to be a powerful propaganda for good will." The reviewer in *Statesman and Nation* commented: "Berto Pasuka has discovered a new art form, which in dance may have an impact comparable with that of African sculpture." The company lasted for six years, touring all over the country. In the television broadcast, which came soon after their first public performance, Pasuka directed two excerpts from their repertoire: 'They Came', which showed the arrival of the white man to Africa and the subsequent clash between Africans and Christians, and 'Market Day', a light-hearted impression of a West Indian market place in which Marie Antia was the Flower Girl. Other women from the Ballet Negres company who took part in the historic television transmission included Pearl Johnson and Marjorie Blackman.

The BBC radio producer Eric Fawcett had been instrumental in bringing together Edric Connor and the London-born contralto Evelyn Dove for an extremely popular radio series called *Serenade in Sepia* (1945-47). When Fawcett began working in the BBC's post-war television service, he decided to bring the series to Alexandra Palace. The television version of *Serenade in Sepia* premiered on 18 July 1946 and made television stars out of Edric and Evelyn. Launching the series, the *Radio Times* described the series as a "sincerely beautiful presentation". The series continued until April 1947 and helped to establish Evelyn Dove as the first black female star of British television in the post-war era. In addition to *Serenade in Sepia*, Edric and Evelyn also worked for Eric Fawcett in a variety special for BBC television called *Variety in Sepia*. This was transmitted live for one hour from Radiolympia at Earls Court twice on 7 and 9 October 1947. It was broken down into five scenes, depicting the story of black song and dance down the years. Eric Fawcett, told the *Radio Times* that he intended to fill the show with the "best coloured talent in the country today" and the line-up he assembled was impressive. In addition to Edric and Evelyn, the first-rate cast included the American dancer and choreographer Buddy Bradley, Trinidadian pianist Winifred Atwell and Cyril Blake and his Calypso Band. Adelaide Hall was prominently featured as the main star attraction towards the end and she sang several classic songs from her repertoire including 'Deep Purple' and 'St Louis Blues'.

The transmission of *Variety in Sepia* that was aired on 7 October has become significant to television history. The final six minutes of Adelaide's performance was preserved by an early process called telerecording. In this segment she sang 'Chi-Baba, Chi-Baba (My Bambino Goes to Sleep)', followed by a medley that included 'I Can't Give You Anything but Love', the song Adelaide had launched in 1928. Before the existence of videotape, no technology existed to record television, but in the 1940s the BBC began experimenting by using a process known as telerecording. This was achieved by filming onto 35mm film stock direct from the television screen as the programme aired. The telerecording of Adelaide's performance in *Variety in Sepia* remained undiscovered in the BBC's archive until 1989 when the author of this book rediscovered it and then screened it at the National Film Theatre in April 1992, with Adelaide in the audience. It is now recognised as the BBC's earliest known recording of a live performance by an entertainer on British television.

In early post-war television, black artists were mainly featured in music and variety shows. However, there were occasional dramatic roles. As early as 1938 the Guyanese actor Robert Adams had played the lead in a BBC television presentation of Eugene O'Neill's melodrama *The Emperor Jones*. Then, on 16 September 1946, Robert Adams returned to television to make his second major appearance in the medium in another famous Eugene O'Neill play, *All God's Chilllun' Got Wings.* This was a complex drama about a mixed marriage, strong stuff for a BBC play in 1946. But the production gave opportunities to two black actresses to appear in the medium. Pauline Henriques was cast as Robert Adams's sister. Interviewed about this landmark production in 1989, Pauline recalled: "I think the BBC pioneered something in giving us a play of that stature to act in. I thought television was wonderful because theatre came into the sitting room of viewers. We only had one television camera and it was static. It was fixed to the studio floor and didn't move! There was also a huge sea of cables all over the studio floor, and I was terrified I would trip over them. We had to remember to keep in shot all the time, and yet a sort of magic came out of this chaos."

Connie Smith was cast as the mother of Robert Adams and Pauline Henriques in this ground-breaking production. Pauline Henriques remembered the veteran actress as "Wonderful." She said that in addition to this television production, "We often worked together in radio and theatre. We always shared a dressing-room, and became quite close. On stage, she had a presence even though she was very small and very quiet. She had discipline and a subtle way of playing a role. I would say she was the first black professional in the theatre I ever met. She would always be on time for rehearsals, and never missed a cue." Connie had travelled from New York to Britain in the 1890s and, together with her husband, Gus, toured for many years as a music hall act. After Gus's death in 1927, Connie made a successful transition from music halls to 'legitimate' theatre, becoming a respected character actress from the 1930s to her retirement in the 1960s. Pauline recalled: “She was always very encouraging to younger actors, especially those of us who were black. I recognised she possessed something very few black actors had back then – enormous experience because her theatrical career spanned from the 1890s to the 1960s.” Connie Smith died in London in 1970 at the age of 95 and she was buried in the Variety Artists’ section of Streatham Park Cemetery in an unmarked grave. Pauline Henriques said this was a fitting resting place: “It doesn’t surprise me that Connie is buried in an unmarked grave because she underplayed everything. She would be perfectly happy with that.”

Sources

Pauline Henriques, interview with Stephen Bourne, Brighton, 4 August 1989

Stephen Bourne, ‘Black Television: Vision on at Last’, *The Wire* (April 1992)

Stephen Bourne, *Evelyn Dove: Britain’s Black Cabaret Queen* (Jacaranda Books, 2016)

Visiting Americans
Part 2

Hilda Simms, star of *Anna Lucasta*, on the cover of *Theatre World* (January 1948)

24 Hilda Simms and *Anna Lucasta*

In 1944, as the star of *Anna Lucasta*, Hilda Simms helped to break down barriers on the New York stage. *Anna Lucasta* was the first American drama with a black cast on Broadway that was not about racism, but a theatre production that focussed on a family at war with itself. Hilda Simms was born in Minneapolis in 1918 and became interested in theatre when she was a student at the University of Minnesota. In 1943, she moved to New York City and joined the American Negro Theatre in Harlem.

The American Negro Theatre (ANT), founded in 1940, became one of the most significant black theatre companies in America between the demise of the African Company in 1823 and the birth of the Negro Ensemble Company (NEC) in 1967. Their constitution drew upon the dictum of the African American civil rights activist W. E. B. Du Bois' that such a theatre company should be *by, about, for*, and *near* African Americans. One of ANT's founder members, Abram Hill, approached a group of librarians and they granted the company the use of the stage in their basement. It was situated in the Harlem Branch of the New York Public Library on 135th Street and Lenox Avenue. By the time ANT staged their most successful production, *Anna Lucast*a, in 1944, they had a following of five thousand. From inauspicious beginnings, ANT blossomed into the most successful black independent theatre of the 1940s.

Anna Lukaska was Philip Yordan's saga of a Polish-American family in Pennsylvania whose daughter is a prostitute. However, when Abram Hill reread Yordan's play, a copy of which he had kept in a drawer for two years, he saw the potential for it to feature an African American family and to lighten the grim, sad drama by transforming it into a comedy-drama. Yordan gave his consent to Hill to change the script anyway he liked, and the production, renamed *Anna Lucasta*, opened on 16 June 1944 with Hilda Simms in the leading role of Anna. It ran for five weeks before a successful theatre producer moved the production to Broadway where it opened at New York's Mansfield Theatre to outstanding critical reviews and huge audiences on 30 August 1944. It ran for 957 performances, finally closing on 30 November 1946.

Ruby Dee later reflected in *With Ossie and Ruby: In This Life Together* (1998): "True, the central character was a streetwalker, and in that respect, the play was in no way ground-breaking, but it was original; it was a fresh look

Hilda Simms on the cover of the first issue of *Checkers* (July 1948), one of Britain's first black magazines. Courtesy of Pauline Henriques

at Negro life, without apology, from a bright, almost sassy perspective. It was a hit in Harlem and immediately attracted Broadway's attention…It was 1944, Broadway needed a lift, needed a laugh, needed to try to forget the war in Europe. *Anna Lucasta* was just the ticket. It opened to rave reviews, and two years later, the show was still playing to full houses. At times, as many as six companies were playing somewhere in the country."

Anna Lucasta made a star of its leading lady, Hilda Simms, who came with the production to London. It opened at His Majesty's Theatre on 29 October 1947 to critical acclaim and popular success. It ran into 1948 for 428 performances. Among the enthusiastic theatre critics was Lionel Hale who, in the *Daily Mail,* said: "Someone has been brilliantly clever, and put the scene in the American family of colour…The whole stage immediately takes on an original life. This is wonderful camouflage of a wildly melodramatic plot; and the audience, hocused by the hokum, was wildly enthusiastic."

The British press coverage for *Anna Lucasta* mainly focussed on Hilda. Reviews for her performance were positive: "beautifully played" (*Times*), "warm and vivid" (*Daily Telegraph*), "Miss Simms is beautiful, vital and possesses the gift of perfect timing" (*Evening Standard*). On 24 November 1947 Hilda was interviewed in BBC radio's *Woman's Hour*. Her photograph appeared on the covers of *Theatre World* (January 1948) and the very first edition of the black British magazine *Checkers* in July 1948. When Edward Scobie wrote about her in *Checkers*, he noted that, after Hilda had left the American cast of *Anna Lucasta*, she studied Shakespeare. Her ambition was to play Juliet on Broadway, but this did not happen. So, she agreed to return to the role of Anna for the London production and decided that it would be a marvellous opportunity to study the reaction to the play outside the USA. He also described her as a young woman "possessed of charm, wit, personality, and a well-informed mind…is fully aware of the obstacles in her path, but like her friend Lena Horne she is a courageous fighter for the rights of all minorities. She is grateful for the warm spontaneous reception which she has received from British audiences."

During her stay in Britain, while acting in *Anna Lucasta*, Hilda devoted some of her free time to various charities. She was invited to address the London School of Economics and at Oxford she gave a lecture on American theatre. She met and befriended the celebrated stage actress Dame Sybil Thorndike and, impressed with the British system of government, she visited Parliament on several occasions. In Oxford, she met a well-known bookseller called Mr Saunders. He took great pride in presenting Hilda with an original photograph of her favourite actress, Eleonora Duse, taken by one of the first British woman photographers, Julia Margaret Cameron. Mr Saunders said: "Please accept this picture of a great actress, to a great actress – I know it belongs with you."

Hilda Simms died in Buffalo, New York on 6 February 1994 at the age of 75.

Source

Edward Scobie, 'His Majesty's First Lady: Hilda Simms', *Checkers*, Vol 1, No 1 (July 1948)

25 Lena Horne: A Lady with Something to Sing About

Lena Horne was an enduring superstar of the entertainment world. Her career spanned more than sixty years, beginning with her debut as a chorus girl at Harlem's Cotton Club in the 1930s, to her one-woman show *The Lady and Her Music* which ran for over a year in New York in the 1980s. By the time she made her first appearance in Britain in 1947, she had been in Hollywood films for several years. In 1942, she had become the first black star to sign a long-term contract with a major Hollywood film studio. The studio was MGM and for them she starred in *Cabin in the Sky* (1943) and made memorable guest appearances in such Technicolor musical extravaganzas as *Thousands Cheer* (1943), *Ziegfeld Follies* (1945) and *Till the Clouds Roll* By (1946). She had also starred in the wartime classic *Stormy Weather* (1943) in which she sang the title song and this became forever associated with her. In the1940s, Lena was one of America's most beautiful and glamorous movie stars and her fame spread across the globe.

In Britain throughout World War II and the rest of the 1940s, movie-goers appreciated Lena's beauty and singing. They recognised that Lena's appearances in MGM musicals marked a departure from the traditional Hollywood stereotype of the black woman as a one-dimensional mammy or maid. The *Monthly Film Bulletin*, published by the British Film Institute, noted in their May 1943 issue that, in *Cabin in the Sky*, "Lena Horne is exquisite as the temptress Georgia" while in their April 1944 issue they acknowledged that in *Broadway Rhythm* "outstanding is the surprising Carmen Miranda type of Latin American number ['Brazilian Boogie'] by Lena Horne." It was the British releases of her film appearances that helped pave the way for the success of her first professional engagement in Britain in 1947.

Lena was born in Brooklyn, New York in 1917 and was greatly influenced by her paternal grandmother, Cora Calhoun Horne, one of the first African American suffragettes. Lena's daughter Gail Lumet Buckley once explained, "If she hadn't had that strength instilled in her by her grandmother she probably wouldn't have coped. Cora gave her that kind of strength that made her survive in many difficult situations where she was terribly exploited and hurt. So many others didn't survive. Look at Billie Holiday, Dorothy Dandridge, Judy Garland and Marilyn Monroe.

Lena Horne on the cover of *Picturegoer* (30 July 1949), a popular British movie magazine

They didn't have the family base or a sense of self."

In 1947, at the height of her movie fame, Lena accepted an offer to travel abroad and make her European debut. Before travelling to Paris, she was booked to appear for two weeks at a popular variety theatre, the London Casino, from 10-22 November. This was situated in the Soho district of London's West End. Lena, accompanied by Ted Heath's orchestra, topped the bill. Also on the trip was Lennie Hayton, one of MGM's top musical directors. They had worked together at the studio, and fallen in love, but inter-racial romances were not acceptable in America. In many states, inter-racial marriages were against the law. So, Lena and Lennie kept their relationship a secret. Before their European trip, the couple decided to marry in Paris, and the happy occasion took place in that romantic city in December 1947. On returning to America they kept their marriage a secret for at least two years, even from their families.

There was no press reception awaiting Lena at Southampton when she arrived on 29 October on the Cunard liner Mauretania, except for two enthusiastic reporters from the *Melody Maker*. This was a weekly jazz newspaper that had been promoting her visit. It seemed the Hollywood movie star's journey to Britain had not been publicised, but on her arrival in London the singer discovered that her appearances in MGM musicals had made her more famous abroad than she had realised. Her many fans included British servicemen from the war who had seen her in films on board their ships and army and RAF bases. Her engagement at the London Casino was a great success. The critics raved about her singing. The drummer Jack Parnell, who performed on stage with Lena in Ted Heath's orchestra, later recalled for her biographer James Gavin, "She used to come in about two hours before every performance to start making up. She became transformed. And on the stage she was absolutely gorgeous to look at."

In her autobiography *Lena* (1966), the singer recalled her impressions of Britain at that time: "I have two vivid impressions of it – the grey coldness of the weather and, in contrast, the tremendous warmth of the people toward Americans. Practically no one had come over from the states to entertain in these early days of post-war austerity. So even though I was not well known, I was given an amazingly warm reception." Lena enjoyed her trip to London: "Mostly it was fun. It made me feel free – freer than I had been in a long time at home. And most of the people we met went to such pains to make us feel welcome." She visited the House of Commons – "to see how real democracy ticks," she told an American reporter.

Lena was given a warm reception in what was one of Britain's worst winters. The country was still recovering from the war. Lena observed the bomb sites across London, and experienced the food shortages. She welcomed a visit from the mother of her friend, the British film actor James Mason. He had instructed his mother to bring her eggs from her small farm in the country. Lena later reflected: "Some wonderful things happened to us. Hilda Simms was there, playing in *Anna Lucasta*, and we spent a lot of time at the digs members of the company had rented." At the parties given by members of the cast of *Anna Lucasta*, Lena met various British writers, actors, painters and the Welsh poet Dylan Thomas. "He was a strange-looking, fey creature," she recalled, "a red, freckled drunk with an odd accent, who kept staring at me and never said anything memorable…I didn't know a thing about him or his fame at the time."

These gatherings also gave Lena opportunities to discuss the situation for black people in Britain. Lena showed a keen interest because she had come face to face with discrimination on her arrival from Southampton at the Piccadilly Hotel in London's West End. Although she was welcomed, Tiny Kyle, her friend and hairdresser, and Luther Henderson, her pianist, conductor and arranger, both African Americans, were not. "There were the usual excuses," she later recalled, "and I made my usual fuss…They got their rooms."

Throughout her stay in London, Lena learned about the growing number of people coming from the Caribbean to live in Britain, especially the cities, and the growing rise in hostility against them. She was also introduced to the hostility of some West Africans towards African Americans. Lena was invited to the West African Students' Union which had been founded in London in 1925. They were a politically active and vocal organisation which campaigned to improve the welfare of West Africans who had come to Britain to study. They also wanted independence for the West African colonies. Said Lena: "I was asked to tell them a little about life in the United States. I could tell from the questions they asked, and from some of the statements with which they peppered me afterward, that they had nothing but contempt for what they regarded as the servility of the American Negro, pity for what they regarded as his attempts to ingratiate himself with white society. They were, they said, going to have freedom in their countries someday soon, and they didn't want to hear about the difference between the conditions in theirs and in the United States. They only wanted to criticise. So naturally we fought violently. I was discovering that travel could be broadening."

Lena never forgot that first trip to London, and there were to be many more, including several appearances at the London Palladium, until 1984, when she brought her Broadway show *The Lady and Her Music* to the Adelphi theatre. Reflecting on that first visit, she said: "Before that trip I was pretty cold on a stage. I sang mostly for myself. What happened in Europe broke down a little barrier I had rigged up for myself. My God, in London, playing a little place in Soho, they were bringing gifts to *me* – gifts when they still needed eighteen coupons for a coat. I cried a lot in London."

Lena Horne died in New York City on 9 May 2010 at the age of 92.

Sources

Lena Horne, *Lena* (Andre Deutsch, 1966)

Stephen Bourne, interview with Gail Lumet Buckley, St George's Hotel, London, 27 May 1987

James Gavin, *Stormy Weather: The Life of Lena Horne* (Atria Books, 2009)

26 Katherine Dunham: A Voyage of Discovery

London, Liverpool, Manchester and Birmingham had never seen anything like it. Katherine Dunham's magnificent dance company had established itself on stage and in films in America, but audiences in post-war Britain were completely unprepared for them. The company arrived in Britain in 1948 and their production, A *Caribbean Rhapsody*, opened to critical acclaim for a three-month engagement on 3 June at the Prince of Wales Theatre in London's West End. It was hailed as London's best musical since Rodgers and Hammerstein's *Oklahoma*! that had opened with great success at the Theatre Royal, Drury Lane in 1947. Company member Eartha Kitt later reflected in her autobiography, *Thursday's Child* (1956): "The Prince of Wales Theatre was the centre and joy of the London theatre district. Ours was the most exciting show that had hit London since the war. London was still grieved from that horror. I could see and feel her wounds." It isn't surprising that *A Caribbean Rhapsody* attracted positive critical attention and packed houses. Katherine Dunham's Dance Company arrived in London when large sections of the city were nothing more than wastelands of bombed out buildings and rubble. Bomb sites could be seen everywhere. It was a depressing time. *A Caribbean Rhapsody* was first class entertainment and did much to lift the spirits of theatre-goers looking for escapism.

In 1979, arts lecturer and critic Dale Harris described the impact of the production in the *Guardian*: "At the height of post-war austerity, London was unexpectedly brightened by the arrival of an all-black revue from the United States called *A Caribbean Rhapsody*, a show with the colourful rhythm and uncanny sense of stagecraft to make it an immediate hit." Katherine had conceived the show as popular entertainment, but she also succeeded in combining a range of dazzling dance styles. In the fourteen episodes, without one word of dialogue, there was jazz dance, born out of the urban black experience; ancient folk ritual; graceful social dances evolved by slaves in imitation of their white masters; American modern dance; and classical ballet. Dale Harris added: "In the midst of the brilliant performers who made up the cast there moved with an unforgettable blend of voluptuousness and imperiousness the star of the entire enterprise, Katherine Dunham, at once choreographer, producer,

VOL. XLIV No. 282 JULY 1948

THEATRE WORLD

Portrait by Maurice

Katherine Dunham

the brilliant and dynamic dancer, choreographer and producer of *Caribbean Rhapsody*, the unique and colourful West Indian entertainment at the Prince of Wales. Katherine Dunham is celebrated from coast to coast in America, and her advent in the West End is an outstanding theatrical event.

3

Katherine Dunham in *Theatre World* (July 1948)

dance historian, university-trained anthropologist and show biz wonder." At the end of each performance, during multiple curtain calls, the audience's wildly enthusiastic applause and cries of joy could be heard as Katherine would prolong the excitement by changing her costume – in a flash – each time the curtain hit the floor. All the costumes in the show, as well as the sets, were designed by Katherine's husband, John Pratt.

The theatre critic for the *Daily Telegraph* attended the opening night performance, and enthused that it "fails almost brilliantly to fall into any known theatrical category... The long-legged and attractive Miss Dunham who was responsible for the excellent production is a dancer of some virtuosity and no mean mime. Her company gave a polished exhibition of teamwork in a variety of dances. Altogether an unusual show remarkable for its artistry throughout."

When *A Caribbean Rhapsody* was reviewed in *Theatre World* the journal praised Katherine as someone who "fills the Prince of Wales theatre with rhythms, colours and a vibrancy seldom experienced on the London stage; she is likely also to fill it with large audiences. Her medium is the dance, and her material is drawn from the coloured peoples and tribal traditions of the West Indies." The following month, Eric Johns wrote at length about Katherine in *Theatre World* after visiting the Prince of Wales Theatre. Johns discovered Katherine one afternoon on stage with her troupe "polishing up the show" and noted that "solo work never interested her. It was the group that mattered, right from the beginning. She is a group conscious individual who only gains satisfaction from using dancers as a sculptor uses clay – to create beauty. She has so little star-consciousness in her mental make-up...She has far more serious thoughts in her head than the flattering of personal vanity...Every performance has to be as near perfection as Miss Dunham can get it...As choreography interests Miss Dunham far more than actual dancing, every dance is devised in detail to a well thought-out pattern, based on authentic steps she has witnessed herself in the Caribbean."

When King George VI and Queen Elizabeth attended a performance of *A Caribbean Rhapsody*, there was some confusion over what Katherine Dunham, an American, should do. Nobody knew whether she should bow, curtsy, lower her head, or forget the whole thing. Eartha Kitt recalled: "We were in our places on stage, watching Miss Dunham's entrance with careful eyes, waiting for her to offer an American greeting to British royalty. On her cue, she came on the stage, almost facing the royal box. She nodded her head in rhythm with the drums, without disturbing the choreography. If one did not know, one would have thought it a part of the dance."

Ballet royalty also took a keen interest in the Company. According to Katherine's biographer, Joyce Aschenbrenner, company members became acquainted with the dancers in the Sadler's Wells Ballet, the elite dancers in London: "Alicia Markova, the prima ballerina of the Ballet Russe de Monte Carlo, introduced them to Margot Fonteyn and Frederick Ashton. They had met Markova and other ballet members in New York. In London, Fonteyn, Ashton, and Moira Shearer started coming to Dunham classes." Company member Tommy Gomez recalled the elation felt by the Dunham dancers in being accepted in London cultural and social circles: "It was so wonderful just to sit across a table in polite British society with someone like Margot Fonteyn. It was such a wonderful relief, being able to relax, and knowing we could go anywhere we wanted to as long as we had the money."

Richard Buckle, the ballet critic for the *London Observer,* described the impact of the Dunham Company on British theatre audiences: "Chiefly it is ballet, but of a quite unusual kind…her bare-footed company made classical dancers seem like waxwork figures… the impact of her company's visit is comparable to the arrival in Paris of Diaghilev's ballet in the year 1908." In 1949 Buckle published a beautifully illustrated photographic record of Katherine and her Company called *Katherine Dunham: Her Dancers, Singers, Musicians*. Roger Wood, a photographer best known for his work in the ballet, provided most of the images, and Buckle described Katherine as "a young woman of charm, wit and purpose, and with the thoroughness, grasp of detail, and determination of a great soldier or explorer, pursuing her studies, enlisting aid and setting forth on a voyage of discovery."

Katherine was one of the first choreographers to give expression to African American experiences and to make a connection with black experiences around the world, especially Brazil and the Caribbean. She discovered that through her art she could reach out to all people, irrespective of their race.

Katherine Dunham died in New York City on 21 May 2006 at the age of 96.

Sources

Dale Harris, 'The dancer who went back to the streets', *Guardian* (7 February 1979)

Joyce Aschenbrenner, *Katherine Dunham: Dancing a Life* (University of Illinois Press, 2002)

27 Eartha Kitt: Five Dollar Fine, Kitty

During her long and illustrious career, Eartha Kitt visited Britain on many occasions, most memorably in 1988 when she took over the role of Carlotta in Stephen Sondheim's *Follies* at London's Shaftesbury Theatre. Every night she stopped the show with 'I'm Still Here' and she followed this triumphant appearance with a memorable return to the Shaftesbury in her one-woman show in 1989. But Eartha never forgot the wonderful reception that greeted the show in which she made her London debut in 1948, *A Caribbean Rhapsody*, with Katherine Dunham and her Dance Company.

Eartha, who had been born in poverty in North Carolina in 1927, had joined the Company in September 1944 at the age of seventeen and she was affectionately known to the other dancers as 'Kitty'. She later recalled that historic trip in 1948: "We all got off the boat at Southampton with the feeling of Alice in Wonderland, but when we arrived in London it was very bleak. The British people were on rations. We were also given ration cards and the people here had a very hard time getting real meat. I experienced feelings of guilt to be eating the meat, butter, eggs and chocolate we had. I felt guilt taking it away from the British people so most of the time I gave my food stamps to somebody in the Prince of Wales theatre, like the ushers, who had elderly parents or children. My chocolate rations always went to the ushers. It was a very interesting time for me because I had come out of the American South which was also a very bleak area of the world for me. So when I came to London that experience that I had from the South also became acute in me because I was walking through the streets of London and seeing blitzed houses and places that had been demolished by bombs, and people without food." As an American who hadn't had to face the horrors of the war, Eartha expressed the shame and guilt that she felt during her stay in Britain: "I was glad that I was born in a part of the world that had been so well protected, but I was also ashamed of my protection. I carried guilt inside for being a privileged character when the rest of the world was being destroyed."

For Eartha, one of the highlights of *A Caribbean Rhapsody* was the opportunity to greet King George VI and Queen Elizabeth when they arrived at the theatre for a performance. She said: "A buzz went through the company that one of the dancers had to greet the King and Queen in a dance number as they came through the lobby. I was more scared than elated when I was the one chosen. I don't remember what happened, except that I was very scantily dressed and wriggled to the sound of four Cuban drummers as the ceremony passed through the lobby of the theatre. I was numb with shyness."

When London theatre critics kept noticing Eartha, Katherine Dunham decided to give her a solo spot: "'Quirino con su tres', I sang, moving across the stage in a rumba-style costume…My costume had frills that trailed the floor and a bandanna had to be worn over my long hair: this was a rule. Since I wanted to show my long curly hair, I put the bandanna as far back on my head as was possible with two or three bobby pins to hold it. 'Five dollar fine, Kitty,' Miss Dunham would say each time she caught me as I came offstage. 'Black people don't have long hair,' she would say." Despite this, young Eartha had nothing but admiration for Miss Dunham: "I would stand in the wings watching this beautiful woman extend her fantastic legs into the air with Vanoy Aikens holding her, moving her, lifting her – the most fantastic thing I had ever seen. I was proud to be in the Katherine Dunham Company. I was learning through watching and observing."

During the long and successful run of *A Caribbean Rhapsody,* Eartha shared a flat in Manchester Square in Marylebone with another cast member, Julie Robinson, who later became the wife of Harry Belafonte. Eartha described the location as a "beautiful neighbourhood", however, Britain's clothes and food rationing forced the two young women to a strict regime: "We gradually became acquainted with people who helped us by telling us where to buy food. We soon felt at home in England…To buy clothes was another problem. We were allowed twelve coupons every three months to buy wools or cashmere, and naturally everything we wanted was wool or cashmere. Nylon stockings were out of the question. No one had any. My Aunt often sent me food and Julie's mother did the same."

Eartha and Julie enjoyed the time they spent in London, and in their spare time they explored the metropolis. Eartha recalled their visit to the Tower of London: "to see the old castle where the guards are dressed in sixteenth-century costumes" and other famous landmarks, "we walked across London Bridge. I had the feeling that any minute the bridge was going to topple. 'London Bridge is falling down, my fair lady'…When we went through Jack the Ripper's playing ground I felt his presence everywhere. Any second he would dart out of a house and grab some damsel by the neck and rip. It was really weird if you went through there at night. When I saw Scotland Yard, I expected Sherlock Holmes and Dr. Watson to walk through the gates. We lived and breathed by Big Ben, the clock everyone looked up to. He never made a mistake." Eartha and Julie also socialised at a popular jazz venue, the Caribbean Club, just off Piccadilly. However, Eartha was upset by some of the sights: "Walking the streets of London and riding in double-decker buses to areas that had been bombed and not cleared or rebuilt yet made me feel so angry. The movie newsreel scenes were nothing compared with the reality. To see a church half blown away, whole areas bombed and left in memory of man's inhumanity to man, would leave me standing in awe and rage."

Eartha also felt anger in Liverpool, the first stop on their tour. She remembered "the uncomfortable feeling I had when I walked the streets. The loathing of the waterfront where the slave boats had docked. This was where it all began, with Africa, across the sea. I used to stand on the pier for hours staring out over the water. Was I feeling sorry for them that are no more, or was it for me, a descendant of them? I was more than happy to leave Liverpool." The Company's next stop was Paris and this is where Eartha decided to jump ship and spread her wings as a solo artist. It didn't take her long to become an international superstar of stage and screen.

Eartha also continued to work in Europe. There were two contrasting highlights when she read Bible stories on Sunday afternoons for the BBC (surely the first black woman to do so), and gave a notorious rendition of 'An Englishman Needs Time' with a flirtatious look at HRH Prince Philip (sitting next to Queen Elizabeth II in the Royal Box) during the Royal Variety Show at the London Palladium.

In 1968 Eartha was invited to a White House luncheon given by President Lyndon Johnson's wife, Lady Bird Johnson. It turned out to be an invitation to disaster. In conversation with the President's wife, Eartha spoke out against the Vietnam war. It was a passionate outburst for which she would pay a very high price for it led to FBI and CIA investigations of both her professional and personal lives. Her career in America suffered for almost ten years. Fortunately, her reputation abroad was not affected. Britain welcomed her back and, in the early 1970s, she made many guest appearances on popular television shows including *Stars on Sunday*, *Russell Harty Plus*, *Parkinson* and *The Good Old Days*, as well as the film *Up the Chastity Belt* with the comedian Frankie Howerd.

Reflecting on her frequent visits to Britain from the 1940s to the 1980s, Eartha later said: "I do not feel British. I feel part of everything, because I have never identified myself as an American or a Britisher or a French person or an Italian. Or a black person or a white person. I belong to everybody or whomever or whatever it is that I fit into at the time, or where I make my home. And that's where my heart is."

Eartha Kitt died in Weston, Connecticut on 25 December 2008 at the age of 81.

Sources

Eartha Kitt, *Thursday's Child* (Cassell, 1956)

Eartha Kitt, *I'm Still Here* (Sidgwick and Jackson, 1989)

Stephen Bourne, interview with Eartha Kitt, Shaftesbury Theatre, London, 21 December 1988

Expatriates Part 4

28 Adelaide Hall: Adopted Daughter of London

After the war, Adelaide Hall continued to tour Britain's variety theatres. In a letter to the author of this book, Michael Lilley recalled seeing Adelaide several times at the New Theatre in Northampton in the late 1940s: "It was widely reported in the national press that she had suffered a burglary and had all her furs stolen. It was the very same day that we saw her in the evening. She walked onto the stage wearing a fur stole. The first words she said was 'This was the only one that they left me!' It brought the house down. I also recall that each time I saw her she sang 'That lucky old sun has nothing to do but roll around heaven all day.' Each time the spotlight would get smaller until at the end of the song only her face was in the spotlight which eventually went out leaving the stage in darkness. The audience loved it."

In the 1940s Rudolph Dunbar, the Guyanese-born musician and conductor, was the London-based correspondent for the popular American newspaper *Baltimore Afro American*. He would report any news stories about black Britons or American expatriates to the paper, so that African American readers could keep up to date with what was happening in Europe. In a 1948 edition of the *Baltimore Afro American*, Dunbar wrote about Adelaide's British successes in a feature entitled 'American-born Entertainer is the Darling of London':

> During the battle of Britain, Adelaide Hall braved the air raids to entertain service troops in England and other parts of Europe, who were defending the last bastion of democracy in Europe. Like other wartime entertainers she had many narrow escapes. Today, Adelaide Hall is a respected and admired adopted daughter of London. She dresses smartly without undue extravagance or ostentation and maintains a beautiful home in one of the most exclusive sections of London. Her next-door neighbour is a titled English gentleman with his family. Adelaide Hall is living in perpetual freshness of youth: her style of singing is vital: and it is no exaggeration to say that she can return to America tomorrow and be in the trend with modern entertainment.

After the 1940s, Adelaide continued working as an entertainer in Britain. In 1988, at the age of eighty-six, she enjoyed a triumphant, sell-out return to New York when she performed in her one-woman show at the Weill Recital Room at Carnegie Hall. In 1989 a Channel 4 television documentary, *Sophisticated Lady*, filmed her in concert at London's Riverside Studios. In 1991 she celebrated her ninetieth birthday by taking part in an all-star tribute at London's Queen Elizabeth Hall. Said Ann Mann in her review in *The Stage*: "When Hall appeared on stage at the end of the concert the crowd went wild…Adelaide Hall's staying power, vivacity and sheer love of the business in which she works, is something which should act as a lesson to us all."

Adelaide Hall died in London on 7 November 1993 at the age of 92.

29 Elisabeth Welch: At Home Abroad

During the war, Elisabeth Welch continued to be featured in West End musicals and revues including *Sky High* (1942) and Ivor Novello's *Arc de Triomphe* (1943). Then came one of Elisabeth's most popular stage successes, *Happy and Glorious*. It opened at the London Palladium in October 1944 where it ran for a record-breaking 938 performances until May 1946. Elisabeth said: "I was so happy working with Tommy Trinder in *Happy and Glorious* at the Palladium. Two shows a day. We were in the theatre about half past eleven in the morning and we got out about seven at night. It was a big revue, very glamorous with lovely dancing girls. We were in the middle of another Blitz. This time Hitler was sending over the V2 rockets, and we just had to cope." After the war, Elisabeth reigned supreme in London's West End in sophisticated revues devised and directed by Laurier Lister: *Tuppence Coloured* (1947) and *Oranges and Lemons* (1948). In *Tuppence Coloured,* which opened at the Lyric Theatre in Hammersmith on 4 September 1947 and transferred to the Globe Theatre the following month, Elisabeth co-starred with Joyce Grenfell and Max Adrian, and introduced to Britain a song she had 'discovered' in Paris:

In October 1946, I went over to Paris, to see what was left of it, and to look up some friends. It was there that I first heard this name, Edith Piaf. Everyone was talking about her and she was playing at a wonderful theatre called the Olympia, an enormous house, so I went to see her. I'll never forget that evening. This little waif appeared on the stage and walked to the centre. There was no glamour, or beauty, but when she opened her mouth you were absolutely fascinated by the passion and the force that came out of this woman. She was so fantastic. Then she sang 'La Vie en rose'. She was a person who loved to be in love, and that year she was in love and so she wrote the lyric to this song. *Tuppence Coloured* was a big success and everywhere I sang 'La Vie en rose', on tour in places like Aberdeen and Liverpool, and then in London, it had a fantastic reception. It is a beautiful song, even if you don't know French. I love the song because it's from the heart, and Piaf sang it from the heart. I'm so proud I introduced it to Britain.

A private person, Elisabeth seldom gave interviews to the press, but she did consent to being profiled at the height of the favourable publicity generated by her appearances in post-war revues. In

S W 3 (25 September 1948), J. Pardoe offered readers an insight into her personality and private life:

Elisabeth Welch's personality is a harmonious one, tuned to the triad of generosity, charm and sparkle. Whoever heard her deep genuine laugh will recognise it as the expression of a generous mind that gives freely, and gladly lets others partake of the gifts which nature gave her. Vivacity, grace and intelligent facility of conversation as well as a gift for listening when her interest is roused, predestine her as the centre of every party. Her exquisitely feminine ways, her chic and elegant appearance, her sparkling yet never adder-sharp wit form a piquant contrast to the childlike, credulous streak which is also part of her mental makeup. She quickly sums up people and has a good insight into human nature. Elisabeth Welch is a staunch friend to her friends, a most loyal and helpful colleague, a gay and ever stimulating companion, but she doesn't like to meet people whom she doesn't like.

After 1948, Elisabeth remained a popular star attraction in London's West End in musicals and revues for many decades. In 1985 she won rave reviews – as well as a nomination for a Laurence Olivier award - for her performance in *Jerome Kern Goes to Hollywood*, an intimate celebration of the composer Jerome Kern. In 1987 a documentary film called *Keeping Love Alive* captured her splendid concert performance at London's Almeida Theatre at the age of eighty-three. Miles Kreuger, president of the Institute of the American Musical, summarised Elisabeth for the *Los Angeles Times* (19 July 2003): "Elisabeth Welch wasn't just another singer; she was a cultural icon, like Ella Fitzgerald is to this country. She could do anything... with the most sweet and plaintive voice, and she had absolutely impeccable diction and taste. In a recording career that began in 1928 and lasted into the 1990s her voice was absolutely untouched by time."

Elisabeth Welch died in Northwood, Middlesex, London on 15 July 2003 at the age of 99.

Sources

Elisabeth Welch, interview with Stephen Bourne, Knightsbridge, London, 15 August 1993

Stephen Bourne, *Elisabeth Welch: Soft Lights and Sweet Music* (Scarecrow Press, 2005)

Britain 1948

30 Pauline Henriques, *Anna Lucasta* and the Negro Theatre Company

Pauline Henriques was thrilled to be an understudy for one of the cast members of an American play called *Anna Lucasta* when it transferred from Broadway to London in 1947. She said: "I felt I was extremely lucky to be an understudy in *Anna Lucasta*. This was an American Negro Theatre production which had come over to the West End with the complete cast. There was an enormous build-up for this American theatre company, and everybody was quite feverish because rumour had it that they were going to have British black understudies. I was thrilled when I got the part understudying Georgia Burke. She was the oldest and frailest member of the cast, but she never missed a single performance! I was one of the understudies who never went on stage. *Anna Lucasta* had a tremendous impact on the British public and we knew almost immediately that the play was going to run."

Pauline had always wanted to act and, in the late 1940s, opportunities began to come her way, even though roles for black actresses were rare. Pauline couldn't sing or dance, so she knew opportunities to act would be limited. However, 1947 was a good year for her. Before understudying in *Anna Lucasta*, Pauline was seen in *Caviar to the General* at the Lindsey Theatre and Noel Coward's *Point Valaine* at the Embassy Theatre. Feeling confident, that same year, in July, she wrote to the BBC and reminded them that she had given an audition for them in 1945. She said: "Since then I have been working hard in the theatre. I have also made several recordings for the *Caribbean Voices* programme. As I am a coloured actress the parts that I can play on the stage are limited and I wonder if I can have another audition (now that I have had much more experience) with a view to seeing if there were any openings in the drama section of the BBC." The BBC replied: "You will appreciate that our auditions waiting list is very long and ever-increasing; and we cannot therefore consider giving any artist a second audition at present." However, Pauline's understudy work in *Anna Lucasta* led her to realising an ambition to put together a showcase for black British talent. It was called the Negro Theatre Company, one of the first black British stage companies.

Pauline was born in Half Way Tree, Kingston, Jamaica in 1914 and, in 1919, at the age of five, she arrived in England with her family and settled in St John's

Wood, London. Pauline's father, Cyril, was a successful import and export merchant who wanted his six children to have an English education. Pauline described him as "a most interesting man. He was well educated, cultured and had a passion for reading, music and the theatre." While growing up in London, Pauline went to the theatre regularly and dreamed of becoming an actress. At the age of eighteen she went to the London Academy of Music and Dramatic Art to study drama for one year. "I started going to the theatre when I was seven," she said. "I lost my Jamaican accent rather quickly, so when I went to drama school I had an English accent, which was perfect for 'classic' roles."

Pauline adored the African American singer and actress Elisabeth Welch who had made London her home in 1933: "I thought she was the most wonderful black person ever. She had grace and beauty, and a tremendous range in her singing voice. She could also act. So, of course, I modelled myself on her and dreamed that, maybe, one day I could be her understudy, but that dream was never realised."

Pauline didn't take up an acting career after leaving drama school and described herself as a "comfortably off" young housewife when the war started. By 1939 she was married to Geoffrey Henebery, an insurance clerk, and they had a two-year-old daughter called Gail. The Henebery family had just moved into a flat in Hampstead when they heard on their radio Neville Chamberlain's famous speech, in which he declared war on Germany. Pauline said: "And then the air-raid warning sounded immediately after Chamberlain's speech, and we thought let's get out." Pauline and Geoffrey climbed up Parliament Hill and watched barrage balloons rising across London: "It was almost magical, although the implications were frightening…It was not really an air-raid warning. I think it was probably done to alert people to the importance of what had happened… In a funny sort of way, we really didn't have any knowledge of what was going to happen, so I don't think we were frightened." Pauline's parents had just returned to Jamaica and, when the threat of war became a reality, they asked her to come and stay with them: "but I felt that my roots were here." Pauline didn't expect to join up: "In those days when you married and had children you stayed at home. I took it for granted this was my role. In any case, at the beginning of the war, I was a pacifist and didn't entertain any thoughts of joining up."

Towards the end of 1939 Geoffrey's employers relocated him to Carlisle, a city in Cumbria, close to Scotland. He took his family with him. Pauline described this as a totally new life, an "absolute revelation." During their first year in Carlisle, Geoffrey was called up and joined the Navy. Pauline

Pauline Henriques

found herself with time on her hands, so she took in three evacuees. At that time, mothers with young children were discouraged by the government from working, though many in this situation demanded to contribute to the war effort. In 1942 some young mothers marched – with placards strapped to their prams and pushchairs – demanding 'We want war work. We want nurseries.' Pauline was one of those young mothers who wanted to undertake war work, even though she was taking care of a young daughter, and the evacuees. She said, "I didn't want just to be the housewife and keep cleaning the whole time. It seemed an unnecessary waste."

Pauline described the young mothers she befriended in Carlisle in the early years of the war as a "little community" who were longing to do something for the war effort: "One or two of them went to the Air Ministry and I thought I could do that, so I taught myself to type." Pauline found employment typing invoices for the Air Ministry. It was the first money she had ever earned, and she was thrilled with the independence it gave her: "Then I found it was just lovely having my own money. I wasn't earning much, but just to be able to control it…I could never think of not earning money again."

Pauline was very popular in her community. She said there were two reasons for this. First, she was the only black person in Carlisle - apart from some African American GIs who were billeted there after the United States entered the war in December 1941 - and second, having a "good speaking voice." During the war, Pauline realised an ambition to work in the theatre by using some of her spare time to act and produce with the Carlisle Little Theatre. This was an amateur theatre company and she said she didn't encounter any racism at all: "Everybody found it an interesting novelty to have a black woman involved. In Carlisle people were surprised to find this intelligent black woman working with a theatre company, keeping busy and active."

Towards the end of her life, Pauline reflected: "There was great relief when the war in Europe was over, but it was short-lived for me because of the shock of Hiroshima. I remember the news of that, and was just shattered by the horror, and what it was going to mean. It was just so, so awful…Deep down I don't think I ever believed that the war was ever right, and I had kept this in my mind all along. I had always, throughout the war, stuck up for the pacifists."

When Pauline left Carlisle in 1944 she moved back to London, but the acting bug stayed with her. She found broadcasting work with the BBC's Empire Service in *Calling the West Indies* and often took part in the popular literary programme *Caribbean Voices*. In 1946 she was cast by the BBC in a television adaptation of Eugene O'Neill's stage drama *All God's Chillun'*

Got Wings. Then, in 1947, came *Anna Lucasta*.

Pauline recalled that, after the understudies had rehearsed their parts for a few weeks, they realised that they were going to have a lot of evenings with nothing to do: "So I thought that it would be a good idea if we – the British blacks who were the understudies – got together and did our own play readings. So we chose one-act plays such as Thornton Wilder's *The Happy Journey*, a rather unusual play about some people going on a journey in a car. We had to do quite a lot of miming, so it was an imaginative production. That was the nucleus of what we were beginning to think of as the British black theatre movement. We didn't actually give ourselves a grand title. Many of us had so little experience in the theatre that we couldn't really compare ourselves to the American actors. But we had good strong voices, and decided to get experience by seeing if we could do this play and put it on as a serious production."

Consequently, Pauline booked a little theatre in Hampstead in north London, and tried out *The Happy Journey* on a Sunday evening. "We were very lucky because we had good support from the *Anna Lucasta* company," she said. "They were really wonderful. They gave us some publicity, came to the show, and got some of their friends to come as well. I think we did something really important with that production. It helped to launch people by giving them the confidence to get on and take parts when they came along."

Next came the idea of staging a more ambitious production. Another *Anna Lucasta* understudy, Neville Crabbe, contributed an article called 'Negro Theatre Company' to the magazine *Checkers* in October 1948 about this venture. Music, dancing and slapstick comedy had been the parts allocated to black artists. Pauline, Neville and their colleagues aimed to change that situation. Public support came from Frederick O'Neal who was in the cast of *Anna Lucasta;* the well-known Trinidadian folk singer Edric Connor; and Dame Sybil Thorndike, who agreed to be the Company's Patroness. Neville told *Checkers:* "It was decided that while the training was of primary importance – it would also be good policy to put on a show to publicise the group and raise funds for the purpose of establishing classes in stage technique. It was agreed that Miss Pauline Henriques, who already had some years' experience as a producer and actress, should produce the dramatic items on this first programme."

The production, a mix of musical and dramatic items, was called *Something Different* and it was staged at Maccabi House in Compayne Gardens, West Hampstead on a Sunday in July 1948. Among the women in the cast were Ida Shepley, who acted in an excerpt from *Golden Boy* and sang spirituals and Mabel Lee, who sang several numbers. Neville Crabbe told *Checkers*: "There were many mistakes made, but many lessons learned. Perhaps the most important of these was the fact that the group learnt to appreciate the value of team-work, and it was this co-operative spirit that they are going to work for in the future."

In their December 1948 issue, *Checkers* reported on a farewell party organised on 31 October 1948 by the Negro Theatre Company before several of its members left to go on tour with *Anna Lucasta.* The evening's entertainment, produced by Pauline, included a mix of songs and dramatic interludes. Songs were provided by Ida Shepley and Rita Stevens, who had been understudying the role of Stella in *Anna Lucasta*. Rita also acted in Eugene O'Neill's 'miniature play', *Before Breakfast.*

In 1950 Pauline realised her ambition to act in a Shakespeare production when Kenneth Tynan cast her as Emilia in a touring version of *Othello*. The African American actor Gordon Heath was cast as Othello. She said: "I loved the excitement of working in the theatre, but I felt I could do better. I had a voice, but it wasn't until Kenneth Tynan cast me as Emilia in *Othello* that I realised what a wonderful thing it was to act in a Shakespeare play on the stage, and to speak those marvellous lines. I eventually gave up acting because I realised it was useless to depend on it for a living, and I needed to have a full-time career." In the 1960s Pauline left the acting profession and turned her attention to social work. In 1966 she became the first black woman in Britain to become a magistrate, and in 1969 she was appointed OBE.

Pauline Henriques died in Brighton on 1 November 1998 at the age of 84.

Sources

Neville Crabbe, *Checkers*, Vol 1, No 2 (October, 1948)

Pauline Henriques, interviews with Stephen Bourne, Brighton, 4 August 1989 and 18 March 1995

Mavis Nicholson, *What Did You Do in the War Mummy?* (Chatto and Windus, 1995)

Jenni Murray, *The Woman's Hour: 50 Years of Women in Britain* (BBC Books, 1996)

31 Winifred Atwell: A Star is Born

The pianist Winifred Atwell enjoyed a meteoric rise to fame in post-war Britain and it soon led her to the top of the 'pop' charts. In addition to becoming the first black recording artist to reach the number one position, 'Winnie' was the first British star to have three records sell over a million copies, and Britain's most successful ever female instrumentalist. Her hands were insured at Lloyds for £40,000 – a vast sum in the 1950s – and her fan club had over 50,000 members.

Winifred Atwell was born in Tunapuna, near Port of Spain, Trinidad in 1915. She was the daughter of Frederick Atwell, a chemist, and his wife Sarah, a district nurse. Winifred began playing the piano at the age of four. Within a couple of years, she was giving Chopin recitals at charity concerts, as her mother Sarah later recalled in an interview in the *TV Times* in 1957: "She never got into mischief as she would play the piano for hours. At six Winnie could play the piano as well as the organ in church, but we had no piano on which she could practice. We'd saved 500 dollars to buy our house, but when dad and I saw how much Winnie needed a piano, we spent the money on a new piano instead. There isn't a sacrifice I wouldn't make for my daughter. Winnie doesn't say it in words, but I know in her heart how glad she is that her piano helps her to make her mummy happy." As a young woman, Winifred worked in her father's chemist shop, and he insisted that she took a degree a pharmacy, but in her spare time she entertained her friends, and continued to take part in charity concerts. It was not until 1937 that she became a professional musician. In 1941 the celebrated classical pianist Alexander Borovsky heard her play and he was so impressed that he advised her to leave Trinidad and go abroad. However, the war prevented this.

After entertaining in Trinidad's Services Club during World War II, as well as touring the Caribbean islands, in 1945 Winifred travelled to New York to study piano technique with her idol, Alexander Borovsky. Winifred gave a recital at the New York Town Hall to great acclaim, but she decided to move to London to study at the Royal Academy of Music. Travelling first-class, Winifred arrived by ship from New York at Southampton on 30 August 1945. Her tutor at the Royal Academy of Music was Professor Harold Craxton and in 1993 his son, Michael, recalled those early days of hope and promise: "Winifred and father got on very well together. Father liked

Winifred Atwell

her sunny, charming personality, and she was always very cheerful. He had great respect for her musicianship and there was a very good rapport between them. Father wouldn't have given her the time that he did if he didn't feel that she was going to be a considerable talent on the concert platform." On arriving in Britain, Winifred lived in a hostel for West Indians, and then she found digs with a kind landlady in Wembley Park. Winifred later told Godfrey Winn in an interview for *TV Mirror* in 1957: "I paid three pounds ten a week out of my allowance. That covered everything, my food as well, even my washing. And I didn't encounter any prejudice."

With a small allowance from her parents, Winifred studied music during the day, and earned some extra money by working in the evenings playing piano in dance halls and clubs. She had been taught the rudiments of boogie-woogie by McDonald Bailey, the Olympic sprinter, who was also from Trinidad. She made an immediate impression and caught the attention of Keith Devon, an important show business agent of the Delfont Agency. After successfully auditioning for him, Winifred was on her way and, on 21 October 1946, she made her BBC television debut in *Stars in Your Eyes*. Her BBC radio debut followed soon after, on 8 December 1946, in *Breakfast Club*.

Stardom followed for Winnie after she married Reginald 'Lew' Levisohn in 1947. He was a variety artist who gave up his stage career to manage his wife's professional engagements. Encouraged by Lew, the shy Winnie was groomed for stardom and quickly became a larger-than-life show business celebrity. In 1997 Nadia Cattouse commented on the relationship: "Off-stage she was a true Trinidadian. Well educated, middle-class, but full of warmth and fun. She fitted in with the English. You had to in those days if you were going to make it. She also succeeded because her husband, Lew Levisohn, had the right contacts, and the 'push'. Through him she became a star and she must have wanted it, because she told people she would put her head in a lion's cage for him. That's how much she loved him and appreciated what he had done for her."

In 1948 Keith Devon booked her for a Sunday charity concert at the London Casino in place of a star who had fallen ill. Winifred was almost completely unknown before the curtain rose but, after captivating the audience with her ragtime music, she found herself taking several curtain calls. The impresario Bernard Delfont immediately signed her to a long-term contract and sent her on a tour of the provincial music halls.

Winifred had no idea what was expected of her in the world of variety. Her first booking was at the Empire Theatre in Belfast, and on the Monday morning she was summoned to something known as a 'Band Call'. All Winifred knew was that she had to be there. The Musical Director asked for her music. "I haven't any," she replied truthfully. "I play from memory." The Musical Director explained that his orchestra had to play too! "All right," replied Winnie, "play anything you like. *I'll* follow *you*." Back in London Winnie had good friends who gave her advice on how to present herself on-stage and build an act. After the music hall variety tour, when she played the London Casino again, she was booked as a twice-nightly attraction, not as a Sunday concert replacement.

Edward Scobie attended one of Winifred's appearances at the London Casino, and described what happened in the November 1948 issue of *Checkers*: "Winifred Atwell walked to a piano in the centre of the stage, adjusted the 'mike' and in a cultured voice explained her act. Without fuss, she treated the audience to a well-balanced mixture of boogie-woogie, Greig concertos and popular melodies. She was a hit...The audience insisted on an encore. She replied with the famous *Fire Song*."

A fellow Trinidadian Pearl Connor-Mogotsi, who arrived in Britain in 1948, recalled in 1993: "She was a quiet, dignified lady. She played that piano very well, but she wasn't playing honky tonk when she first came to Britain. That was unheard of! When she showed how expert she was, Winnie married Lew Levisohn, an entrepreneur, a promoter, and he brought her out of herself. On-stage, with Lew's support and direction, she changed completely. She became a different person. All that stuff with the honky tonk, pounding away at the Palladium, that was somebody else. Off-stage she became that quiet lady again. It was quite an experience seeing Winnie make these changes. Everything she did on-stage was an act. When you saw her on-stage you'd think she was an uninhibited extrovert."

In the bleakness of the post-war years, the British public took her straight to their hearts and a star was born. Her success was sealed in 1951 when she signed a recording contract with Decca, which led her to the top of the charts, and on 3 November 1952, an appearance in the first Royal Variety Performance for the new Queen, Elizabeth II. To a rapturous reception, Winifred closed her act with the number she'd composed specially for the occasion, 'Britannia Rag'.

As Roy Plomley's guest in BBC radio's *Desert Island Discs* (1952), Winifred asked if she could be cast away on "one of those little uninhabited islands in the West Indies" where she could build a hut. "I could make quite a pretty one out of plaited coconut strips – and I'd make a roof out of carat palm leaves." She told Plomley that she could survive quite easily on green coconuts, mangoes, sapodillas, plantains, avocado pears, fish and land crabs. "There's a fish called cascadura," she added. "You catch it in shallow, muddy water. I'd boil that with green plantains and wild peppers and bay leaves. Delicious! I could make my cooking utensils out of calabash shells. There'd be the most gorgeous flowers just for the picking, and humming birds flying around." Plomley interrupts, "All right, Winifred, there's no doubt about you having won your Castaway's Badge, First Class, with honours."

Said Pearl Connor-Mogotsi: "Though some of us who came from Trinidad knew her, and her family, she never got mixed up in the general movement of assisting our people, or exposing herself to politics. She wasn't that kind of person anyway. She kept herself to herself right to the end of her life. But she broke down barriers in her own way with her expert piano playing and when she opened one of the first hairdressing salons for black women in Brixton. She was a credit to us all. We were very proud of her."

Winifred Atwell died in Sydney, Australia on 27 February 1983 at the age of 67.

Sources

Checkers Vol 1, No 3 (November 1948)

Michael Craxton interview with Stephen Bourne, London, 20 July 1993

Pearl Connor-Mogotsi interview with Stephen Bourne, London, 26 July 1993

Nadia Cattouse, interview with Stephen Bourne, London, 1 January 1997

32 Pearl Connor-Mogotsi: The Mother of Us All

In post-war Britain, Pearl Connor was a force to be reckoned with. Her passion and energy for raising the profile of Caribbean arts and culture led to the creation of work for black actors, writers and film-makers. Several ground-breaking initiatives included the founding, in 1956, of Britain's first theatrical agency for African and Caribbean actors. In the early 1960s Pearl was the driving force behind the formation of one of Britain's first black theatre companies, the Negro Theatre Workshop.

Pearl was born Pearl Nunez in Diego Martin, Trinidad in 1924. Her father, Albert Nunez, was a headmaster and her mother, Georgina, a teacher. Pearl described her childhood as "lovely, magical, folklore-based" and she said her greatest influence was Beryl McBurnie, a Trinidadian who was dedicated to promoting the culture and arts of the island. Beryl was the founder of the Little Carib Theatre, where Pearl gained her first acting experience. Also in the 1940s she helped to organise the Trinidad and Tobago Youth Council with Beryl. The Youth Council was responsible for the Caribbean Youth Conference in 1947.

Pearl wanted to study journalism in America, but an uncle who lived there advised her father that America was unsafe for a young woman. Pearl was still in Trinidad in February 1948 when Edric Connor visited his homeland. Edric was a folk singer and actor who had journeyed from Trinidad to Britain in 1943 and had achieved a great deal of success and popularity, mostly on BBC radio and with recordings such as 'The Lord's Prayer'. By 1948 he had become a national hero back home and, on his return, Pearl was selected with another girl to accompany him as couriers on his tour of the island. "We admired him, of course," she said, "and we were very proud to be with him. That's how I first met him."

Disappointed at not being allowed to study in America, Pearl was encouraged by Edric to come to Britain as there were opportunities to study there. Pearl later recalled in *Horizons: The Life and Times of Edric Connor* (2007): "Father was quite happy because he thought England was a safe country. He did not know much about it." Pearl journeyed from Trinidad on the ship Ariguani and arrived in Bristol on 14 April 1948 and she then travelled to London to study law. She said: "The spring was

Edric and Pearl Connor's wedding day in London (1948). Courtesy of Milverton Wallace and the George Padmore Institute

a multi-coloured carpet of wheat, corn and other crops. We arrived at Paddington Station where Edric sent his secretary to meet me. She was an Englishwoman, and was quite kind and helpful." Edric offered Pearl a room in his flat in Lancaster Gate, and took her on a sight-seeing tour of London "and to see the lights of Piccadilly Circus." Edric assisted Pearl in obtaining information about universities. She recalled: "Edric and I began to know each other better, and to grow closer. I was a great admirer of his work and his commitment to our culture and liberation, and found him to be a kind and understanding person. He was concerned for me to get on with my studies."

Pearl appreciated Edric's insistence on promoting Trinidad and Caribbean culture by singing their folk songs whenever he could: "He was an expert on our folk dances, which he taught me. Father never allowed us too near the native culture. When calypsonians went past our house, father would call us in and close the shutters. He wanted us to have a good English education and to emulate the British way of life. For the first time I heard from Edric about calypsos, Carnival, the dances and songs. I thought he was on the same wicket as I was, just the right person for me." Pearl described Edric as an avid student: "A self-made person. He read widely. He had a great collection of books on all sorts of subjects. He embraced literature, music and so on. He was self-taught. He was always learning. Always practicing and developing his art. He was a perfectionist and believed in what he was doing. He wanted to be the best." When Pearl arrived in London in 1948, apart from Edric, she didn't know any other Trinidadians in the country, "except for an old family friend, Frank Singuineau, who was an actor. One felt isolated and in need of close friendships."

Towards the end of the war, and immediately after, the British government tried to show some appreciation for all the people from the colonies who had contributed to the war effort. Said Pearl: "Those little Caribbean islands had all stuck their necks on the block. Some of our young men had gone and died. My own brother joined the Royal Air Force and flew a Lancaster bomber over occupied Europe. He was killed in action in 1943. The British government wanted to show some appreciation. There was an open-door policy. They weren't locking us out, yet. The BBC were also interested in helping to promote the Caribbean people. So Edric came to Britain at a good time. Doors were open to him. He didn't have to kick too hard. It was relatively easy for Edric to attract attention. But it didn't last. By the 1950s we had become second-rate citizens."

Within three months of her arrival, Edric asked Pearl to marry him. She accepted and they were married in London on 26 June 1948. Pearl was twenty-four at the time. Said Pearl: "I did not know Edric very well, only as a celebrity of Trinidad and Tobago. He came from a totally different background to mine. In a way I felt isolated, as there were so few of us in London. When he proposed to get married, I thought that I was of an age to marry and he was quite a suitable person. It was like an arranged marriage, and I decided he was the right person for me, as we had so many interests in common."

Pearl experienced racism for the first time when she accompanied Edric on their honeymoon in Eastbourne. On their arrival at the hotel they were informed that no booking had been made, and that no room was available. "You can imagine how upset I was," Pearl recalled. "However, Edric contacted his agent who had made the booking, and after much coming and going, the manager came out and apologised profusely. Then we were given a room. That was one of the worst nights of my life, and I could not wait to leave the next morning and return to London." Pearl said that Edric had not experienced racism before, having been 'protected' by his friends and colleagues in show business since his arrival in Britain during the war. Said Pearl: "I was part of his first experience of overt prejudice."

Edric Connor believed in the liberation of the colonised people of the British Empire and, through her husband, Pearl became more interested in and involved with Caribbean politics. She said that she only found out about the Jamaican nationalist Marcus Garvey when she began studying in London, and mixed with politicised people from other Caribbean islands and Africa, and those who also lived in nearby Notting Hill Gate, which in 1948 had become the centre of African and Caribbean settlement in London.

With Edric, Pearl met and befriended some of the great names in the worlds of black arts, politics and culture in post-war Britain. Edric was a great admirer of Paul Robeson. Said Pearl: "We all admired him, and thought he was one of our greatest artists, and a great man. Edric hero-worshipped him. Paul was Edric's role model and Edric wanted to be like him. So, not long after we were married, when Paul came to England for a concert tour, Edric invited him to our house for tea. I remember thinking our tea set wasn't up to scratch, so I had to rush out and buy a new china tea set! On important occasions, or for a celebration in our culture, we must have something special, and I wanted a new tea set. For me that was important, but I don't think Paul Robeson even noticed, he was too busy talking to Edric!"

Reflecting on her work as a theatrical agent, Pearl recalled: "We struggled for years because the pay for our artists was low. We didn't have named artists on our books, we didn't have people with great reputations, we were building reputations. And that was our pioneering work. We were breaking stones and it was very tough." The Jamaican actor and film-maker Lloyd Reckord, who arrived in Britain in the early 1950s, described her as a "guardian angel" to all young black actors in Britain: "Her home was always open to people like us. She'd even let us sleep on the floor until we could find a place to live. And she just worked continually, pushing black actors, quarrelling with the powers-that-be, arguing 'Why can't black actors get this sort of part?'" In the BBC television documentary *Black and White in Colour* (1992), the actress Carmen Munroe acknowledged Pearl's contribution to Caribbean arts: "Pearl made things happen for us. She took chances. She took risks. She pushed, and we learnt a lot from her, and from the way she handled situations. Pearl was the mother of us all, a great lady, and we are all very grateful to her."

Pearl Connor-Mogotsi died in Johannesburg, South Africa on 11 February 2005 at the age of 80.

Sources

Stephen Bourne, interview with Pearl Connor-Mogotsi, London, 13 July 1989

Roxy Harris and Sarah White (editors), *Changing Britannia: Life Experience With Britain* (New Beacon Books, 1999)

Edric Connor, *Horizons: The Life and Times of Edric Connor* (Ian Randle, 2007)

Mona Baptiste's arrival on the Empire Windrush on 22 June 1948. Courtesy of Alamy

33 Women on the Windrush

On 22 June 1948 the *Empire Windrush* docked at Tilbury in Essex bringing with it the first wave of post-war settlers from the Caribbean. The British Nationality Act had just been passed and this gave the status of citizenship of the United Kingdom and Colonies to all British subjects residing in the United Kingdom or a British colony. Many ex-servicemen from Jamaica, Trinidad and across the Caribbean who had served in the war took the opportunity to return to Britain, and have a better life, while others were inquisitive and wanted to make the journey to see what life was like in the 'Mother Country'. There were complaints from some members of parliament, but the first legislation passed to control immigration did not happen until 1962. Said Lynne Macedo in *The Oxford Companion to Black British History* (2007): "The arrival of the *Empire Windrush* is viewed as a turning point in the recent history of Britain, and has come to symbolise the many ways in which Caribbean people have contributed to and transformed aspects of British life." More recently, in *Black and British: A Forgotten History* (2016), David Olusoga has described the arrival of *Windrush* as "a great watershed in the black history of Britain and the year she arrived has come to be seen as the symbolic beginning of the modern phase in the relationship between Britain and the West Indies."

In all, around 500 settlers (492 passengers and several stowaways) landed at Tilbury. One of the passengers was the Jamaican Sam King who had served in the RAF in wartime and wanted to return to England and make his home here. He later recalled: "Caribbean immigration to this country really started with that boat. As we got closer to England there was great apprehension in the boat because we knew the authorities did not want us on land. So, we knew we were not wanted but, being British, once we arrived at Tilbury everything humanly possible was done to help us." A number of calypsonians also journeyed to England on the *Windrush* and these included the Trinidadian Lord Kitchener who was filmed arriving at Tilbury. The now famous Pathe newsreel not only records the arrival of the *Windrush* passengers, but features a youthful Lord Kitchener singing 'London is the Place for Me', which he had written on the ship.

When the story of the *Windrush* passengers is told, in newspapers, books and in television documentaries, it is usually the story of the men who

Mona Baptiste

came, mostly from Jamaica, but some from other parts of the Caribbean such as Trinidad. However, there were some black West Indian women on the *Windrush,* but their stories have been almost airbrushed from the narrative of this historic event. On his arrival Lord Kitchener made an impact with his calypso song, which he then recorded, but his presence overshadowed another singer who arrived on the *Windrush*. The Trinidadian Mona Baptiste arrived in Britain the day after her twentieth birthday. As far as the immigration officials were concerned, Mona was a clerk, but in fact she was a singer who hoped to have a career in show business. She gave her intended London address as Penywern Road SW5 (Kensington and Chelsea), but in the 1948 Electorol Register she entered her address as nearby Collingham Gardens. Mona pursued a singing career almost as soon as she arrived. She made her BBC radio debut with the calypsonian Lord Beginner in *Tropical Magic* on 9 August 1948 and quickly followed this with *Band Parade* on 16 August. She also sang at Quaglino's Restaurant in London's West End. However, Mona found greater success and popularity in Germany where she based herself in the 1950s and for most of her career. She was described as 'Europe's Queen of Calypso'. Mona died in Krefeld, Germany on 25 June 1993 but her story remains almost absent in the *Windrush* narrative.

Before the 1950s, other ships brought black women from the Caribbean to Britain including fifteen on the *Reina del Pacifico* in January 1949. Most came to work in hospitals, but it wasn't long before women in the Caribbean were being recruited by London Transport and British hotels.

Thanks to the Windrush Foundation it is possible to access some interviews with passengers from the *Windrush* on their website and these include Lucilda Harris. She was born in Jamaica and had married a tailor, Parnell Adolphus Harris, who had migrated to England in 1947. It was Lucilda who, with several other passengers, helped to hide a stowaway after she was discovered on the *Empire Windrush* seven days after leaving Kingston, Jamaica. Her name was Evelyn Wauchape, a thirty-nine year-old dressmaker from Jamaica. A whip-round was quickly organised on board the ship and £50 was raised – enough to cover her fare and leave her with £4 pocket money.

When Parnell had saved enough money to send for his wife, he and his brother met her when she landed at Tilbury on 22 June 1948. It was a surprise to her when he told her that he would be taking her to live in one room in Somerleyton Road, Brixton. There were many other West Indians who settled in Brixton, near the marketplace, so Lucilda felt at home. Although she was unhappy about living in one room, she was very glad to be with him again. Soon afterwards, he brought her a fur coat, which she wore for more than fifty years.

Lucilda and Parnell raised a family of five children and played their parts in making Brixton a happy place in which to live. They were always ready to help other West Indian settlers after they arrived in the 1950s. Parnell worked as a Master Tailor, making uniforms for the Metropolitan Police.

Parnell died in 1977 but before she died in 2001, Lucilda gave an interview to a BBC website about her journey to Britain on the *Empire Windrush:*

Imagine how exciting it was for me. It was a big troop boat and you have lots of soldiers and lots of people coming to England. There were lots of men on the *Windrush,* more men than women, but what I can remember now, there was a woman that stowed away on the boat. They found her and she got VIP treatment. When I came to England I live in Brixton, near the market. My husband sorted out a place to live, before he sent for me. Well, when I was in Jamaica they said this is a very dark country. The houses were all smashed because of the war. It was 1948 and the war had finished. Anyway, we get together and started having our children. I have no regrets about coming here, because my family is all here, all what I am interested in is here. Bringing up my children and looking after my husband, that's occupied my time. He went home to Jamaica and come back and took sick and he died, and I couldn't just pick myself up and go home and leave my kids here like that. Well, I am glad that my husband sent for me, anybody come to this country they can make a good life, it's a nice country. It cold, it's different, but you can live happily. That's all I'm saying. I'm only sorry he is not around. But I live a good life, a clean life, and I am pleased with it.

For some women who were part of the 'Windrush Generation', life in the 'mother country' was harsh, but the women were strong and resourceful. They coped with adversity. Interviewed in *Forty Winters On* (1988), Lynette Findlater, a dressmaker from Jamaica, who arrived here age twenty-five in 1951, recalled her first job in England in a jam factory: "When I finally got a job I had to work twelve to fourteen hours a day in horrendous conditions for less than the white workers." When Lynette complained, she was sacked. When Albertha Blackman-Thomas arrived from Guyana in 1961, she also found the going tough. Interviewed in *The Motherland Calls: African Caribbean Experiences* (1989), she recalled the time she was offered a cleaner's job, even though her passport stated that she was a teacher: "I remembered a poem, 'The Two Crossing Sweepers', and one of the verses said: *Though poor, they were too proud to beg/Too upright to steal/And gladly did they sweep and clean/To gain an honest meal.* So I took it."

Isolyn Robinson left Jamaica in 1954 to live with an aunt in Geneva Road, Brixton. Her first job was washing up at Lyon's Corner House in Piccadilly. When Isolyn was interviewed for *Forty Winters On*, she said: "Sometimes people would say to me 'Do you think this country is a goldmine?' I just told them, 'All my life in Jamaica I've been drilling up and down in front of the Union Jack and I've got a right to be here." Isolyn summarised what most settlers felt when they arrived here: "Some white people were very nice to me and gentle, some weren't too bad and some were nasty. Day by day I met the lion, the tiger and the teddy bear."

Sources

Forty Winters On: Memories of Britain's post-war Caribbean Immigrants (Lambeth Services; *The Voice* and *South London Press*, 1988). Reissued in 1998 as *The Windrush Legacy* by the Black Cultural Archives.

The Motherland Calls: African Caribbean Experiences (Hammersmith and Fulham Ethnic Communities Oral History Project, 1989)

Stephen Bourne, 'Sam King', *Speak of me as I am: The Black Presence in Southwark Since 1600* (Southwark Council, 2005)

Lynne Macedo, 'Empire Windrush', David Dabydeen, John Gilmore and Cecily Jones (editors), *The Oxford Companion to Black British History* (Oxford University Press, 2007)

David Olusoga, *Black and British: A Forgotten History* (Macmillan, 2016)

www.windrushfoundation.org

BBC History, 'Windrush – Arrivals' (www.bbc.co.uk)

Student Nurses Constance Nelson and Monica Munroe of Grenada at Fulham Hospital (1945). Courtesy of Imperial War Museum (Ref: PL9609F)

34 National Health Service

The National Health Service (NHS) was established in 1948 to provide free and accessible health care for everyone. Almost as soon as it was launched, labour shortages led to intensive recruitment campaigns in Britain and overseas. In the colonies, such as British Guiana, the Caribbean and West Africa, this recruitment drive attracted many black women who came to Britain to help build the NHS. Advertisements appeared in the nursing press and in a number of Caribbean newspapers and journals. British hospitals needed qualified nurses, trainees and domestic workers, though most of the black recruits were channelled into low-paid ancillary and auxiliary jobs within the NHS. However, some of them were successful in becoming nurses. They were pioneers, brave and defiant, but they were not the first, for there had been some black nurses working in British hospitals and related professions since the Victorian era, though information about them is hard to find.

The most famous black nurse from British history, and one who has been honoured with an English Heritage Blue Plaque, a portrait on public view in the National Portrait Gallery and a statue erected outside St Thomas' Hospital in Lambeth, is the mixed-race Jamaican/Scottish 'doctress' Mary Seacole (1805-1881). Mary had tended to soldiers on the battlefields of the Crimean War in the 1850s, but there are a handful of other pioneers who are not as well known.

Frances Batty Shand (1815-1885), the mixed-race daughter of a white Scottish plantation owner in Jamaica and his long-term partner, a free Jamaican woman, was also born in Jamaica. Frances moved to Scotland in childhood and was instrumental in founding the Cardiff Institute for the Blind in 1865. Annie Brewster (1858-1902) was born on the Caribbean island of St Vincent and in 1881 she was living in Camberwell, London with her father, a Barbadian merchant and her step-mother. Annie was employed as a nurse at London Hospital from 1881 until she died in 1902.

However, by the 1930s, black women like Annie Brewster who wanted to work as nurses were not welcome in British hospitals. The 1932 Annual Report of the League of Coloured Peoples (LCP) referred to the Jamaican nurse Eva Lowe who, though well qualified, had been rejected from British hospitals many times. Eva finally found a position at the London County Council Hospital, St Nicholas in Plumstead. Her father collected more than twenty rejection letters and one of them was reprinted in the LCP's Annual Report: "It is not the colour we personally object to, but it is the very difficult time the girl would have with other nurses…I have a young and enthusiastic class of women, numbers of whom are Army men's daughters and whose prejudices are very strong. I am afraid for the girl because she might be ostracised and then she would be so unhappy."

The July-September 1934 edition of the newsletter of the LCP, known as *The Keys*, published a report from the *News-Chronicle* (15 June 1934) about a young black woman who came to England to train as a nurse. She was rejected by all of the twenty-eight hospitals she applied to. The newsletter also reported that LCP member Una Marson had addressed the British Commonwealth Conference in London and informed them that, "No hospital, however, will willingly admit that there is a ban against coloured nurses, but after talking to a number of hospital matrons, secretaries, and governors I learned that a coloured girl has a very poor chance of securing a nursing post in the average hospital." The newsletter continued: "Several hospital officials admitted that while they had no objections to coloured nurses they had to consider the feelings of patients who might strongly object. One secretary said: 'While we have no official colour ban,

Nurse Ademola at Guy's
Hospital, London

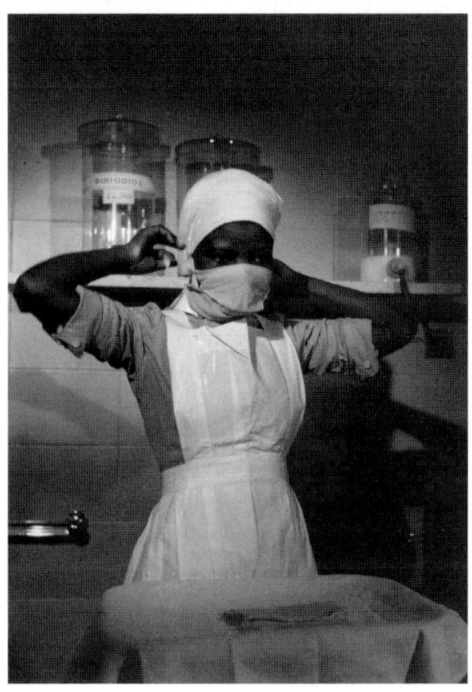

no coloured girl would stand an earthly chance of becoming a nurse with us.'"

An exception was made for the daughter of the exiled Emperor of Ethiopia, Haile Selassie. When Italy made war on his country and invaded it in 1936, he fled to England with his family. He spent his exile years in Bath, Somerset while his daughter Princess Tsehai, the Ethiopian word for Golden Sun, trained as a nurse at London's Great Ormond Street Hospital for Sick Children. The children loved her and she graduated as a State Registered Nurse on 25 August 1939 and served in London during the Blitz of 1940/41. After the liberation of Ethiopia by the Emperor's own army and by British and allied forces in other Ethiopian campaigns, the Emperor requested that his daughter return home. On 19 February 1941, Princess Tsehai made the following BBC broadcast: "I've come to know England, and that means to love it; but duty calls me to my own country...The sympathy and kindness showered on us during our exile will be an abiding and blessed memory, and our hearts will go out to you across the world. In my own language I say to you, Igzabair Yistilingual that means May God Reward You." The Princess returned to Ethiopia with a unit of British Red Cross nurses to initiate the work for the health services of her people. However, she died on 17 August 1942 from complications during childbirth. Emperor Haile Selassie founded the Princess Tsehai Memorial Hospital in her memory, which also served as a nursing school.

There is evidence from a handful of photographs in the collection of the Imperial War Museum that some West Indian women worked as nurses in London during the war. They are named, and some of the hospitals are identified, but the stories of these pioneers are not known. Some information has come to light about a Nigerian nurse. Her name is Princess Ademola and she had come to Britain before the war to train at Guy's Hospital. The Princess was the daughter of the Alake of Abeokuta, the paramount chief of Northern Nigeria, and she had journeyed with him to England in 1937 to attend the Coronation of King George VI. The chief, who was interested in hospital services and hygiene, decided that his daughter should train as a nurse in England, and to specialise in midwifery. At Guy's Hospital she qualified as a State Registered Nurse and remained in London for at least part of the war because, in 1943, she was the subject of a short documentary film produced by the Colonial Film Unit, now thought lost.

The National Health Service came into existence on 5 July 1948 and it is recognised as one of the major social achievements of Britain in the twentieth century. It changed people's lives because, for the first time, British people could access health care completely free at the point of delivery, no matter what their social status and without the need for any assessment of their income. Before 1948, people either paid for their health care or went without. People had to pay for doctors, hospitals and medicines. In many working-class communities, where money was scarce, the very poor could have hospital care for free, but they had to undergo a humiliating means test.

The new NHS was far costlier than anyone could have expected but there was a strong desire for it to succeed. From 1948 the British government funded recruitment drives to attract qualified nurses, trainees, domestic workers and other staff into the hospitals. Recruitment took place in Britain and overseas. The response from British-born women was poor. During the war women had flocked to nursing as part of the war effort. Afterwards most married women returned to the home to raise families.

Recruiting from the Caribbean began in 1949 and Ann Kramer (author) and Abigail Bernard (interviews) captured some of the post-*Windrush* experiences of Caribbean women in the nursing profession in their superb book *Many Rivers to Cross* (2006). One of the contributors was Tryphena Anderson, a Jamaican who left her island for England in December, 1952. She trained as a nurse at Nottingham General Hospital, where she worked as a junior nurse. There followed psychiatric nursing at the Coppice Hospital, also in Nottingham. In 1966 she qualified as a midwife and that year she became the first black person to receive a bursary to train as a health visitor. In 1988 Tryphena bought a nursing home, which she ran until 2002. In September 2012, Tryphena joined the Nottingham Black Archives' Council of Elders. Tryphena told Abigail Bernard: "I opted for nursing. My main influence – beside my mother wanting the best profession for her children – was my cousin who was the health visitor at one of the district's health centres [in Jamaica]." Tryphena's first impressions of England were "Oh god how dreary!" But the biggest shock of all for Tryphena was seeing ordinary white people doing ordinary work. In Jamaica she said you were made to believe that the English were aristocrats, "that they didn't clean floors and they didn't sweep streets. I couldn't understand any of what they were saying! Frankly, I think I spoke better English than most of them!" Tryphena didn't care for English food: "The beef was raw and it was stringy! I couldn't get used to beans. There was no spice; everything was cooked different." She looked forward to trying a dish called Welsh Rarebit because she had never eaten rabbit before: "When I got to that dining room guess what it was? Cheese on toast!"

Others who were interviewed by Abigail Bernard for *Many Rivers to*

Cross included Lucy Martin-Burnham who also travelled from Jamaica in 1951 aged just nineteen: "I was on the boat for fourteen days. I was the only black person and found it a little strange. It was a mixture of excitement in that I was going in uncharted waters but there was a job at the end." Lucy trained as a nurse in Amersham General Hospital, Buckinghamshire and in 1956 she qualified as a midwife and a year later became a health visitor. After arriving here, Lucy found it "quite strange really because I suppose I was comparing England with Jamaica: the brightly coloured buildings, nice and clean looking, then I came into this docklands and it was very drab and in a way I was disappointed. It was quite different to what I expected."

Louise Garvey, who came to England from Jamaica in 1957 at the age of fifteen, originally worked in a cotton factory but she wanted to become a nurse and started training as a cadet nurse at Congleton Hospital, Cheshire. She qualified as a State Registered Nurse and progressed to the position of sister. She told Abigail Bernard that her early years in the NHS were good, "because people sort of got on and supported one another," but that patients and staff could be racist. Louise didn't let anything hold her back. She set her sights on becoming a sister. She did extra training, but obstacles were sometimes put in her way. She felt that black nurses were only there "to do the bedside things. I used to do what I called the watching game. I would watch and see what training was available, who was going for it and how often. I used to challenge the situation. I would say nurse A and B she's had x amount of training, I haven't been on one. This training is available and I am interested, here is my application and that's how you got on these things in those days. You had to fight for them."

Erena Kydd was born in St Vincent and she was twenty-two when she came to England in 1959. Her first job in the NHS was an auxiliary in the Queen Elizabeth Hospital, Birmingham. She was given a job on the wards, but felt more like a domestic than a nurse: "They were saying 'You go and clean the toilets and the bedpans'. In those days nurses had to go on their knees and scrub the floors. I wasn't allowed around the patients. I said 'I didn't come here to clean bedpans. I left my home and I came to this country and I thought I would better my position, but this, I've never done it at home.'" Though Erena had to overcome many difficulties and challenges, she remained committed to the NHS until she retired in 1992.

The story of Daphne Steele is one of dedication, hard work and success. Daphne travelled from her home in British Guiana to London in 1951 and recalled, for Tony Sewell in *Keep On Moving: The Windrush Legacy* (1998) that, when she became a nurse, discipline in hospitals at that time was almost military. "You all but saluted," she said. "We were the soldiers and sister was the sergeant major." When faced with difficult patients, Daphne said she used a "charm offensive" to disarm any racist intent. She admired Jamaican nurses for "they didn't stand for any nonsense. We use to have Jamaican nurses fighting our battles. If a nurse felt that someone was bullying her, a Jamaican nurse would say point me in that person's direction." In 1964 Daphne became Britain's first black matron, at St Winifred's Hospital, Ilkley, West Yorkshire. "I earned that job," she said. "It was not a token appointment." Looking back for Tony Sewell, Daphne said that she believed that the nurses who came to Britain from the Caribbean brought something different to the NHS: "Dedication, the compassion of our culture, joy and commitment." Daphne died in 2004.

Sources

Elyse Dodgson, *Motherland: West Indian Women to Britain in the 1950s* (Heinemann Educational Books, 1984)

Beverley Bryan, Stella Dadzie and Suzanne Scafe, *The Heart of the Race: Black Women's Lives in Britain* (Virago, 1985)

Delia Jarrett-Macauley, T*he Life of Una Marson 1905-65* (Manchester University Press, 1998)

Tony Sewell, *Keep On Moving: The Windrush Legacy* (Voice Enterprises, 1998)

Abigail Bernard and Ann Kramer, *Many Rivers to Cross: The History of the Caribbean Contribution to the NHS* (Sugar Media, 2006)

Jenny Douglas, 'National Health Service', *The Oxford Companion to Black British History* (Oxford University Press, 2007)

Stephen Bourne, *Mother Country: Britain's Black Community on the Home Front 1939-45* (The History Press, 2010)

35 Hostilities in Liverpool

In the port of Liverpool after World War II, history repeated itself when black workers were identified as the scapegoats for unemployment. This had already happened just after World War I, and led to the 1919 'race riots' in Britain's seaports. After World War II, redundancies and unemployment led to resentment from white citizens and Liverpool's black community once again found itself being targeted. Despite being part of the Liverpool community for generations, and having just contributed to the war effort in the services and war factories, black Liverpudlians were seen as "foreigners", "strangers" or "aliens". Widespread unemployment in the seaport, particularly in shipping, provided the spur to anti-black hostilities. The fierce competition for jobs prompted the National Union of Seamen (NUS), under firm right-wing domination, to try and keep black seamen from working on British ships.

In *Black Salt* (2012), Ray Costello said: "The once-welcomed black contribution to the merchant navy was now resisted by the National Union of Seamen, which had made a determined effort to keep black seamen off merchant ships since the end of the war...At the union's annual conference in 1948, the assistant general secretary boasted that in several instances they had been successful in changing ships from black to white crews...This policy led to physical attacks on black people in Liverpool, whether they were seamen or not." Costello added that those black men who tried to defend themselves by retaliating found themselves open to hostile police action, since the police focused their attention on the black minority rather than the white majority.

In 1948 Liverpool's black community numbered about 8,000, most of whom had come to Britain during the war to support the war effort. Of the 8,000, about 30 per cent of the black adults were seamen, and another 10 per cent had jobs on shore, in the docks. The other sixty per cent of Liverpool's black population were unemployed because of the 'colour bar' being practiced by the National Union of Seamen. The hostilities led to a climax during the Bank Holiday weekend of July/August 1948 when a white crowd between 200 and 300 from the area known as the "South End" gathered outside an Indian restaurant and attacked a West African as well as the restaurant. On the second day the situation escalated when a crowd estimated at 2,000 attacked Colsea House, a hostel for African and Caribbean seamen in Upper Stanhope Street. When bricks were thrown through the window, the seamen barricaded themselves in. Black clubs and cafes as well as black individuals were also targeted, but Liverpool's black community quickly retaliated. Some of them either remembered or had been told about the 1919 'race riots'. Fights broke out between black and white citizens but, when the police intervened, those arrested were predominantly black. Fuelled by misreporting in the newspapers, and misleading statements from the magistrates and judges, the public perception was that black people had started the conflict. Fifty black people were arrested and charged but a response from the black community can be found in the report of the Liverpool Colonial People's Defence Association: "It then became necessary that the men held should be defended. Coloured people all over the country became alarmed at that development and wondered how it would end. Support came from London and Manchester. This group and some others formed a working committee which eventually became known as the Colonial Defence Committee which did all that it was able to do in defence of the men." The report refers to the men who were subjected to violence and police harassment and arrest, but at least two black women were arrested by the police. Rene Martis age 24, a pianist, and Ruth Mann age 25, a factory worker, were charged with obstructing the police. At court they were found not guilty.

Liverpool's black community leaders, keen to bring an end to the hostilities, as well as police victimisation, called a meeting at Stanley House, a black community centre. The police were invited to send a representative, which they did. But great harm had been done to race relations in Liverpool, and it was not easily forgotten. Then a group of white citizens, calling themselves the Liverpool Advisory Committee, was set up to monitor the situation of the black community on Merseyside. The Committee sent a report to the Colonial Office with recommendations that, where possible, black seamen should be discharged from the Merchant Navy and that unemployed black people who were claiming the dole should be repatriated. This report further divided Liverpool's black and white communities, and its threatening tone led to the Colonial People's Defence Association working harder than ever to help broaden the struggle for the rights of Liverpool's black citizens.

In August 1948, while the West Indians from the *Empire Windrush* were settling into their new jobs and making a home for themselves in the 'Mother Country', Liverpool's black community were forced to relive the horrors of 1919. Said David Olusoga in *Black and British: A Forgotten History* (2016): "As the next chapter in the black history of Britain was beginning, Liverpool was reliving the nightmare of 1919...organised attacks on the homes and clubs of black people."

Sources

Anthony H. Richmond, *Colour Prejudice in Britain: A Study of West Indian Workers in Liverpool 1941-1951* (Routledge and Kegan Paul, 1954)

June Henfrey and Ian Law (editors), *A History of Race and Racism in Liverpool 1660-1950* (Merseyside Community Relations Council, 1981)

Peter Fryer, *Staying Power: The History of Black People in Britain* (Pluto Press, 1984)

Carlton Wilson, 'Liverpool's Black Population During WWII', Black and Asian Studies Association Newsletter 20 (January 1998)

Ray Costello, *Black Salt: Seafarers of African Descent on British Ships* (Liverpool University Press, 2012)

David Olusoga, *Black and British: A Forgotten History* (Macmillan, 2016)

Conclusion

Black British citizens have always had to fight for equality and justice. In 1998 it was addressed by Pearl Connor-Mogotsi when she was interviewed in BBC Radio 2's *Windrush* series *Their Long Voyage Home*. Pearl described what it was like when she arrived here from Trinidad in 1948: "We didn't have any embassies here. We had no representation. We had King George VI and the streets of gold. We came to the mother country but she wasn't a mother. She was a step-mother which makes it worse. You know the history of step-mothers? The relationship was not what we thought it would be.
We looked for an embrace and it didn't come."

However, in *Their Long Voyage Home*, Brenda Clough acknowledged an embrace which came from the church. Brenda travelled from British Guiana to London with her family in 1959. The church offered them much needed support and guidance. Though many settlers faced hostility in the mother country, it was the church that proved to be their true mother in protecting them. Brenda said: "When you come from a church background you brought a letter of reference from your church back home. We went to the Brethren Church in Guyana, so we found a Brethren Church here in London. That letter was given to them and they were really wonderful people and they made us feel at home. The Brethren Church gave us the support we needed and our faith helped us to cope and to focus on the good things to balance things out. Otherwise our lives would have been so miserable."

Not Forgotten

Cherry Adele
was a dancer who began her career with the Ballets Negres company in 1946. She toured with the company for several years and was also featured with them on BBC television. She was the 'Principal Dancer' on the London stage in the musical *Calypso* (1948) and was seen with Audrey Hepburn in a children's Christmas Party revue at the Cambridge Theatre on 9 December 1949.

Amy Barbour-James
(1906-1988). Born in Acton, London to middle-class Guyanese parents, Amy worked as a civil servant and concert singer. She was inspired by her politically active father, John Barbour-James, to become involved in Britain's civil rights movement, and she joined both the African Progress Union and League of Coloured Peoples (LCP). In 1942 Amy became the secretary of the LCP, an important post she held for several years.

Louise Bennett
(aka Miss Lou) (1919-2006). Jamaican poet who championed Jamaican Creole as an artistic medium. Louise appreciated and respected English literature, but she was concerned that Jamaican dialect was not being used by writers. In the 1940s her "dialect verses" were published in Jamaican newspapers and they were extremely popular with readers. In 1945 she was awarded a British Council scholarship to the Royal Academy of Dramatic Art (RADA) in London. At RADA, when she played the Nurse in *Romeo and Julie*t, she did so using Jamaican Creole and was highly commended. After graduating in 1947, she returned to Jamaica. During her two years in Britain, Louise often broadcast to the Caribbean on the BBC's Empire Service. Her obituarist, Mervyn Morris, described her in the *Guardian* (1 August 2006) as "A warm and generous person…loved and respected not only by Jamaicans at home and abroad but also by a wider international constituency." In 2005 Louise's life and career was celebrated on BBC Radio 4 in the documentary *Miss Lou at RADA*.

Georgia Burke
(1878-1985). African American character actress who played Theresa in *Anna Lucasta* at His Majesty's Theatre in London in 1947-48. She later repeated the role in the 1958 American film version starring Eartha Kitt. She died in New York City at the age of 107.

Rita Cann
(1911-2001). Born in Purley, Surrey,

Rita's father was a West African merchant and her mother was English. In the 1940s Rita was an accomplished pianist who led her own Latin American band in London society. In 1942, using the professional name Rita Lawrence, she played the lead in a BBC radio musical play called *Minnie from Trinidad*. It was based on the song Roger Edens had written for Judy Garland to sing in the Hollywood musical *Ziegfeld Girl* (1941). In 1943 she joined the band of the Cuban pianist Don Marino Barreto and played troop concerts. In 1946 she formed her Havana Sextet and spent three years at the exclusive Thameside Bray Hotel, playing Latin rhythms for dancing. Rita eventually left music to work as a telephonist at the British Museum. Her obituarist, Val Wilmer, wrote in the *Guardian* (10 May 2001): "As a black woman she was aware of the importance of personal presentation and always cut a dignified figure, dressed in chic, well-tailored clothes. She retained elegant pre-war manners and speech, but also had a fine sense of humour; recalling the day she and Paul Robeson put the world to rights, she gleefully commented 'I was very Red!'"

Cicely Dale
was an actress who had small roles in films (*Men of Two Worlds*, 1946) and on stage (*Calypso*, 1948).

Evelyn Dove
(1902-1987). Born in London to a Sierra Leonean father and an English mother. After training at the Royal Academy of Music, Evelyn hoped for a career on the concert platform but in the 1920s cabaret and the variety stage was more welcoming. During the 1940s Evelyn entertained the troops and the British public on the variety stage and BBC radio. She had her own radio series *Serenade in Sepia* (1945-47) which transferred to the BBC's post-war television service (1946-47). In 1948 Evelyn starred in the West End musical *Calypso*. Evelyn's long and eventful career in show business is documented in Stephen Bourne's lavishly illustrated biography E*velyn Dove: Britain's Black Cabaret Queen* (Jacaranda Books, 2016).

Evelyn Ellis
(1894-1958). African American character actress who played Gordon Heath's mother Bella Charles in *Deep Are the Roots* at the Wyndham's theatre in London in 1947. Earlier she had created the role of Bess in the original Broadway production of *Porgy* (1927), a role she repeated in the London version at the Prince's theatre in 1929.

Carmen England
(1909-1991). Born Carmen Maingot in Port of Spain, Trinidad, Carmen travelled to England in 1945 with her friend Winifred Atwell. In 1947

Carmen married William ('Paul') England around the time the Colonial Office appointed him as the manager of the British Colonial Club near St Martin's Lane. This is where Carmen opened a hairdressing salon for black women, possibly the first of its kind. Her friend Winifred Atwell opened another in Brixton in the 1950s.
In 1948 Carmen was filmed at the Colonial Club for a British Pathe newsreel called *Hairdressing*. Later, Carmen opened another salon called Carmen Colonial Hairdressers in South Kensington which became a popular meeting place for black women in London. Post-war, Carmen earned a reputation as one of the most successful black businesswomen in Britain. In the 1950s she was also one of the founders of the Notting Hill Carnival.

Pep Graham
(1899-?). Born in Liverpool to a Sierra Leonean father and an Irish mother, Phoebe Zausa Williams took the stage name Pep Graham. She was a featured dancer in a succession of black-cast British shows from *Going Some* (1924) to *Harlem Comes to Town* (1951).

Sadie Hopkins
(1894-1994). Born in Liverpool to a West Indian father and a mother of Filipina/Irish descent, Sarah Francesco took the stage name Sadie Hopkins and worked as a singer and dancer from the 1920s to the 1940s. In 1947 she emigrated to America and became an American citizen in 1956. She eventually returned to Britain and died in Cwmbran in Gwent, Wales shortly before her hundredth birthday.

Mabel Lee
(1921-   ). African American dancer who began her career in 1940 in New York City. From 1944 Mabel spent over two years entertaining the troops with U.S.O. shows. She also travelled with the first black cast U.S.O. show that toured throughout Europe. Mabel always wanted to visit Britain and, in 1947, she successfully auditioned in New York for a revue at the London Palladium. The young jazz tap dancer and singer couldn't contain her excitement. She opened at the London Palladium with the popular comedian Tommy Trinder in *Here, There and Everywhere* on 5 April 1947 and the show ran for nine months. In London she befriended the African American choreographer, Buddy Bradley, who had opened a successful dance school. During her time in London, Mabel taught swing and jive to some of Buddy's pupils. Mabel remained in London to co-star with Edric Connor and Evelyn Dove in the musical *Calypso* in which the tall, slender dancer with the provocative smile stole the show with her charm and vivacity. Her meteoric rise to fame in Britain was covered by the magazine *Checkers* in 1948. They described Mabel as "The Discovery of 1948" and she told them "I love London

Eseza Makumbi

dearly, and I've grown very used to it. I love making people happy."

Eseza Makumbi
(1919-2014). East African housewife discovered in Uganda by the Irish novelist Joyce Cary. He had been commissioned to write the screenplay for *Men of Two Worlds*, a feature film set in Africa. Cary recommended Eseza for an important acting role in the film, even though she had never acted professionally. On 28 October 1944 Eseza arrived in Liverpool on board the Castalia with her husband, Thomas Makumbi, a schoolmaster. While Eseza was filming at Denham studios, Thomas took courses at London University. In the Castalia's passenger list, Eseza entered her profession as 'housewife' and her London address as c/o Thorold Dickinson, Two Cities Films, 15 Hanover Square, London. Dickinson was the director of *Men of Two Worlds* which was released in 1946. He cast Eseza as Robert Adams's sister, Saburi, and she gave a fine performance. In his review in *The Spectator* (26 July 1946), Basil Wright praised her "beautiful voice" and her "beautiful looks". Sadly it was her only acting role. In later years, Eseza became involved in politics and, as an advocate of women's rights and the education of girls, she became the first woman member of the Ugandan Parliament.

Carmen Manley
(1922-). Jamaican actress and playwright who married Douglas Manley in Kensington, London in 1946. Douglas was the son of Norman Manley, Jamaica's Prime Minister from 1959-62. Before returning to Jamaica in the 1950s, Carmen's London stage roles included *Native Son* (1948) and on BBC television she appeared in *The Ship* (1949), based on a short story by H. E. Bates.

Helen Martin
(1909-2000). African American character actress who played Honey in *Deep Are the Roots* at the Wyndham's theatre in London in 1947. Helen had a long and successful career in America and was best known there for her roles in two popular television sitcoms *Good Times* (1974-79) and 227 (1985-90).

Dinah Miller
(1916-1993). Born in West Ham, London to a black mother (of Caribbean descent) and a Welsh father, Winifred Briggs took the stage name Dinah Miller. She was a popular band singer of the 1930s and 1940s who also made recordings and appearances on BBC radio. Because of the Nazi invasion of Europe, Dinah was unable to leave Sweden in 1940 but she continued to record in that country and, based in Stockholm, she sang in hotels and clubs throughout the 1940s.

Connie Smith

Christine Moody

(1914-?). Born in Peckham, London, Christine was the oldest child of Dr Harold Moody, the Jamaican community leader who founded the League of Coloured Peoples in 1931. Educated at Mary Datchelor Girls' School in Camberwell, after qualifying as a member of the Royal College of Surgeons in 1938, Christine joined her father at his surgery in Queen's Road, Peckham. During World War II, Christine became an officer in the Royal Army Medical Corps. In 1944 she took charge of the British Military Hospital in Ambala, Punjab and, after the war, she spent ten years in Ghana as senior medical officer with the Ministry of Health, developing maternity, paediatric and public health projects throughout the country. Christine eventually settled in Jamaica.

Norma Quaye

(1922-). Born in Kent, Norma Quaye joined the Auxiliary Territorial Service (ATS) in 1939. She was the mixed-race daughter of Caleb Jonas Quaye, born in Accra, Ghana, who worked as a musician and bandleader under the name Ernest Mope Desmond. After he was killed in a railway accident in 1922, Norma's mother took her to live in Portsmouth. Her mother was killed in an air raid in Portsmouth in 1941. Her brother was the jazz singer and pianist Cab Kaye (1921-2000). During the war, in 1943, Norma married the Nigerian Dr J. T. Nelson-Cole.

Olga Rhodes

qualified as the first Nigerian female radio engineer having completed a technical course in England (Source: League of Coloured Peoples Newsletter, March 1946)

Connie Smith

(1875-1970). African American music hall entertainer and character actress. In the 1890s she made Britain her home with her husband Gus Smith and they became a popular double-act in music halls until his death in 1927. Connie then made a successful transition to character actress in the 1940s, and her many stage roles included Addie in the London production of Lillian Hellman's *The Little Foxes* (1942). Other 1940s stage work included the London productions of *Three's a Family* (1944), *Stage Door* (1946) and *Hattie Stowe* (1947). She was also a pioneer of post-war BBC television (see 'Television is Here Again') and, after 1947, she toured as Bella for many years in repertory productions of *Deep Are the Roots.* Connie continued acting into the 1960s. From the 1930s to the 1960s, including World War II, Connie lived in Brook Drive in Lambeth close to the heavily bombed Elephant and Castle. Connie died in London on 11 May 1970 at the age of 95 and she was buried in an unmarked grave in the Variety Artists' section of Streatham Park Cemetery.

Gladys Taylor

Born in Jamaica, Gladys was an actress and singer who broadcast for the BBC's Empire Service in wartime programmes like *West Indian Christmas Party in London (*1940) and the popular series *Calling the West Indies* with a fellow Jamaican, Una Marson. She also had occasional bit parts in films like *Men of Two Worlds* (1946). Gladys continued acting in Britain after the war and into the 1970s.

Viola Thompson

(1888-?). Born in Bonthe, Sherbro Island, Sierra Leone. In the 1911 Census she is recorded as a border at Cambray House (now Cheltenham Ladies' College) in Gloucestershire. In the 1930s she was a member of the Executive Committee of Dr Harold Moody's League of Coloured Peoples. In the 1940s she turned to character acting and was featured as Robert Adams's mother in the film *Men of Two Worlds* (1946) and on the London stage in Richard Wright's *Native Son (*1948). Viola vanishes from the records after 1948.

Rita Stevens

had a long and varied career in show business but vanishes from the records after 1958. Most of her childhood was spent travelling with her mother in shows all over Britain. During the war she entertained the American troops for the American Red Cross. She also appeared as a dancer in a London revival of *Show Boat* (1943). Ambitious to 'cross-over' into drama, Rita understudied the role of Stella in *Anna Lucasta* on the London stage (1947-48). She was also a member of Pauline Henriques' Negro Theatre Company in 1948.

Ethel Waters

(1896-1977). Legendary African American singer and actress. Ethel rose to fame during the 1920s Harlem Renaissance as a blues and jazz singer but, in the 1930s and 1940s, she made a successful transition to Broadway - and then Hollywood - with leading roles in revues and musicals. In 1944 she co-starred with Paul Robeson, Canada Lee and the folk singer Josh White for the BBC in Langston Hughes's 'ballad-opera' *The Man Who Went to War.* The cast recorded it in New York for broadcast in Britain. The recording was thought lost until rediscovered in 2010 in America's Library of Congress.

Josie Woods

(1912-2008). Born in Canning Town in London's east end, Josie's father was from the Caribbean island of Dominica and her mother was British with gypsy ancestry. Keen to dance from an early age, she made show business her career. In the 1940s she teamed up with another dancer, a Nigerian called Willie Payne, and they became a popular double-act called 'Josephine and Payne'. They toured in variety and enjoyed engagements in clubs such as the Blue Lagoon.

Appendix I: Black Women in British Cinema 1939-48: A Chronology

1939 (17 October)
British Paramount News.
Newsreel featuring Adelaide Hall in a variety concert at the RAF Station in Hendon entertaining servicemen and women with 'I'm Sending You the Siegfried Line to Hang Your Washing On'.

1940 (8 January)
Pathetone Presents Behind the Blackout.
British Pathe newsreel featuring Adelaide Hall and her Nigerian accompanist Fela Sowande at the Florida Club in London.

1940
The Thief of Bagdad.
With Adelaide Hall and Cleo Laine (as an extra, somewhere in the Bagdad market!)

1942
Gibraltar.
Short lengths of film taken in Gibraltar with a view to making a documentary about the island. It was never completed. Elisabeth Welch and, amongst others, Beatrice Lillie, Edith Evans and John Gielgud, who were there to entertain the troops, are seen visiting Rock Gun (Northern Peak). The footage is now in the collection of the Imperial War Museum.

1942
This Was Paris.
Melodrama with Elisabeth Welch as a cabaret singer.

1942
Alibi.
Melodrama with Elisabeth Welch as a cabaret singer.

1943
Nurse Ademola.
Colonial Film Unit short featuring Princess Ademola from Nigeria training to be a nurse at Guy's Hospital.

1943
West Indies Calling.
Ministry of Information documentary featuring Una Marson presenting *Calling the West Indies* at BBC Broadcasting House.

1944
Hello! West Indies.
Ministry of Information documentary featuring Una Marson. A revised version of the 1943 film *West Indies Calling.*

1944
Fiddlers Three.
Musical with Elisabeth Welch.

1944
Two Thousand Women.
Drama about British women interned in a Nazi concentration camp includes at least three black women amongst the extras.

1945
Dead of Night.
With Elisabeth Welch as the Parisian nightclub owner in the classic 'Ventriloquist's Dummy' segment.

1946
Men of Two Worlds.
Melodrama set in West Africa with supporting roles played by Viola Thompson, Eseza Makumbi and Cicely Dale.

1947
London's Nightworld.
British Pathe short featuring a sequence filmed in the Caribbean Club in London's West End. African Caribbean patrons, including several women, are seen enjoying themselves and dancing to the jive music of the Club's band.

1948 (12 January)
Hairdressing.
British Pathe short with the Trinidadian hairdresser Carmen England filmed washing and styling African women customers in her salon at the Colonial Club in London.

1948
A World is Turning.
Six reels of unedited 'rushes' are all that remain of an unfinished documentary film about Britain's black community. Adelaide Hall is seen in multiple 'takes' rehearsing at home and performing at London's Nightingale Club. Geni Ransome-Kuti, from West Africa, is seen dancing. In the black British magazine *Checkers* (July 1948) the Trinidadian pianist Winifred Atwell was announced as one the participants, but there is no film of her in the 'rushes'. The 'rushes' are now in the archive collection of the British Film Institute.

Appendix II: Black Women on British Television 1946-48: A Chronology

17 June 1946 (first transmission)
Television is Here Again (documentary)
Elisabeth Welch

24 June 1946
Ballets Negres (dance)

18 July 1946 to 28 April 1947
Serenade in Sepia (music)
Evelyn Dove

16 September 1946
All God's Chillun' Got Wings (drama)
Pauline Henriques, Connie Smith

30 August 1946
Starlight (music)
Minto Cato

1 October 1946
Starlight (music)
Minto Cato

21 October 1946
Stars in Your Eyes (variety)
Winifred Atwell

21 January 1947
Close Up (music)
Adelaide Hall

23 January 1947
Starlight (music)
Adelaide Hall

26 January 1947
Variety on View (variety)
Adelaide Hall

5 February 1947
See For Yourself (variety)
Ida Shepley

8 February 1947
See For Yourself (variety)
Ida Shepley

9 February 1947
Stars in Your Eyes (variety)
Winifred Atwell

24 March 1947
Burnt Sepia (revue)
Adelaide Hall, Josie Woods

18 May 1947
You Can't Take It with You (comedy)
Connie Smith

14 July 1947
Stars in your Eyes (variety)
Adelaide Hall

7 October 1947
Variety in Sepia (revue)
Mabel Lee, Evelyn Dove, Winifred Atwell, Adelaide Hall

19 January 1948
Eric Robinson Invites Some Friends to Entertain You (music)
Adelaide Hall

17 April 1948
Saturday Night at the Palace (variety)
Mabel Lee

19 May 1948
Black, Brown or Beige (revue)
Ida Shepley, Spadie Lee (aka Lily Jemmott)

26 June 1948
Café Continental (music)
Josephine Baker

29 June 1948
The Josephine Baker Show (music)
Josephine Baker

10 July 1948
Stars in Your Eyes (variety)
Mabel Lee

8 August 1948
Starlight (music)
Adelaide Hall

28 August 1948
Rooftop Rendezvous (variety)
Maxine Sullivan

4 October 1948
Television Variety Presents Artists Entirely New to You (variety)
Winifred Atwell

1 December 1948
Sepia (revue)
Mabel Lee, Evelyn Dove

Left to right: Anni Domingo, Stephen Bourne, Cleo Sylvestre and Shirley Patterson at Stephen's graduation ceremony at the Royal Festival Hall in 2017. Courtesy of Robert Taylor

About the Author

Stephen Bourne is a writer, film and social historian specialising in black heritage and gay culture. As noted by the BBC among others, Stephen "has discovered many stories that have remained untold for years." Bonnie Greer, the acclaimed playwright and critic, says: "Stephen brings great natural scholarship and passion to a largely hidden story. He is highly accessible, accurate and surprising. You always walk away from his work knowing something that you didn't know, that you didn't even expect."

Stephen was raised in Peckham. He graduated from the London College of Printing with a bachelor's degree in film and television in 1988, and in 2006 received a Master of Philosophy degree at De Montfort University on the subject of the representation of gay men in British television drama 1936-1979.

After graduating in 1988, he was a research officer at the British Film Institute on a project that documented the history of black people in British television. The result was a two-part television documentary called *Black and White in Colour* (BBC 1992), directed by Isaac Julien, that is considered ground-breaking. In 1991 Stephen was a founder member of the Black and Asian Studies Association. In the 1990s he undertook pioneering work with Southwark Council and the Metropolitan Police that resulted in the founding of one of the first locally-based LGBT forums to address homophobic crime. Since 1999 he has been a voluntary independent adviser to the police. In 2002 Stephen received the Metropolitan Police Volunteer Award "in recognition of dedicated service and commitment to supporting the Metropolitan Police in Southwark."

In 1991, Stephen co-authored *Aunt Esther's Story* with Esther Bruce (his adopted aunt), which was published by Hammersmith and Fulham's Ethnic Communities Oral History Project. Nancy Daniels in *The Voice* (8 October 1991) described the book as "Poignantly and simply told, the story of Aunt Esther is a factual account of a black working-class woman born in turn of the century London. The book is a captivating documentation of a life rich in experiences, enhanced by good black and white photographs." For *Aunt Esther's Story*, Stephen and Esther were shortlisted for the 1992 Raymond Williams Prize for Community Publishing. In 2008 he researched *Keep Smiling Through: Black Londoners on the Home Front 1939-1945*, an exhibition for the Cuming Museum in the London Borough of Southwark and that same year he worked as a historical consultant on the Imperial War Museum's *From War to Windrush* exhibition.

In 2013 Stephen was nominated for a Southwark Heritage Blue Plaque for his work as a community historian and Southwark Police independent adviser. He came second with 1,025 votes. In 2014, Stephen's book *Black Poppies: Britain's Black Community and the Great War* was published by The History Press to coincide with the centenary of Britain's entry into World War I. Reviewing it in *The Independent* (11 September 2014), Bernadine Evaristo said: "Until historians and cultural map-makers stop ignoring the historical presence of people of colour, books such as this provide a powerful, revelatory counterbalance to the whitewashing of British history." For *Black Poppies* Stephen received the 2015 Southwark Arts Forum Literature Award at Southwark's Unicorn Theatre.

In 2016 Stephen's acclaimed biography of the singer Evelyn Dove, *Evelyn Dove: Britain's Black Cabaret Queen,* was published by Jacaranda Books and in 2017 came *Fighting Proud: The Untold Story of the Gay Men who Served in Two World Wars* for I B Tauris. In 2017 Stephen was honoured by Screen Nation with a special award for his documentation of black British film and television, and later that same year he was awarded an Honorary Fellowship by London South Bank University for his contribution to diversity.

For further information go to www.stephenbourne.co.uk

Selected publications

Aunt Esther's Story (ECOHP, 1991)
Brief Encounters: Lesbians and Gays in British Cinema 1930-1971 (Cassell, 1996/Bloomsbury, 2016)
A Ship and a Prayer (ECOHP, 1999)
Black in the British Frame: The Black Experience in British Film and Television (Cassell 1998/Continuum, 2001)
Sophisticated Lady: A Celebration of Adelaide Hall (ECOHP, 2001)
Elisabeth Welch: Soft Lights and Sweet Music (Scarecrow Press, 2005)
Speak of Me As I Am: The Black Presence in Southwark Since 1600 (Southwark Council, 2005)
Ethel Waters: Stormy Weather (Scarecrow Press, 2007)
Dr. Harold Moody (Southwark Council, 2008)
Butterfly McQueen Remembered (Scarecrow Press, 2008)
Mother Country: Britain's Black Community on the Home Front 1939-45 (The History Press, 2010)
The Motherland Calls: Britain's Black Servicemen and Women 1939-45 (The History Press, 2012)
Black Poppies: Britain's Black Community and the Great War (The History Press, 2014)
Evelyn Dove: Britain's Black Cabaret Queen (Jacaranda Books, 2016)
Fighting Proud: The Untold Story of the Gay Men who Served in Two World Wars (I B Tauris, 2017)

Stephen's contributions to the *Oxford Dictionary of National Biography* include the following women who are featured in *War to Windrush*

Amanda Ira Aldridge
Winifred Atwell
Lilian Bader
Esther Bruce
Avril Coleridge-Taylor
Pearl Connor
Evelyn Dove
Adelaide Hall
Pauline Henriques
Connie Mark
Ida Shepley
Connie Smith
Elisabeth Welch

Index